Slampig
The Girls You Pass Up, I Pick Up

Pile

NA, Massachusetts, USA

This book is dedicated to Brownie

The Slampig

Everyone remembers a slampig. She was the girl at parties that would get annihilated and sneak off into an empty room with different guys. Then, late night would come and the real party would begin. All the respectable girls would go home for curfew and it was the slampig's time to shine. But it was the kind of shining that looked more like what goes on at a strip club in Montreal. Her top would be off and she could be coaxed into doing some kind of lewd act with a bottle of Boones Farm. In the morning, she would wake up and try to tell whoever was crashed out on the floor how drunk she was, just so they'd excuse her for getting naked and blowing five guys. I know you remember her; after she blew you, she took your ugly friend's virginity.

When you got older, you stopped going to random parties and began the bar scene instead. After all the good looking chicks finished their free Captain and Diets and went home to raid the fridge, you hit on the fatty in the corner. At last call, when you laughed at her jokes and touched her leg, she looked at you like you were a big bucket of chili cheese fries, waiting to be ravaged.

Even if they have a face full of acne scars, there is a certain glamour to a slampig. They are there for you and you are there for them. You both have a no-strings-attached sex deal where getting off is the only goal. The slampig doesn't just provide a free nut; she provides spontaneity and a sitcom-style story for your friends to laugh about.

But sleeping with too many slampigs can be a bad habit. You forget about the good girls, and it may leave you alone and desperate. If you're looking for love, sometimes holding off on that gutter trash at the bar sucking down a frozen mudslide is the best thing to do.

1

Baby Momma

I didn't deserve to graduate high school. In the four years I was there, I had accomplished nothing. I barely went to class, barely passed a test and worst of all, never got laid. My self-esteem was at an all-time low and even though I was relieved to have escaped high school, graduating a virgin made me feel like a failure.

When all my jock buddies went to their Ivy League colleges and my stoner friends went to work in their manual labor jobs, I went to community college. Community college is basically post-high school purgatory. The one good thing about it was that those girls didn't already know me as the kind little virgin they could talk to about their problems. The bad thing was that the girls in community college were trashy, and you shouldn't put a lot of stock into them. The outcome could be disastrous.

I took a girl named Dana from my Basic Reading class on a date to Friendly's. After she ordered a chocolate Fribble, she gave me the run down on her life. Dana had no job and lived at her grandmother's apartment with her four-year-old daughter Crystal. I was so desperate for any kind of female attention, I turned the caution light off and proceeded with the date.

After the date, we had nothing to do, so I brought her back to my father's house. We started kissing and things started to get heavy. I took Dana's shirt and bra off and she lay down on her back. "Why don't you go down on me," she whispered.

I unbuttoned her tight jeans and pulled them and her lacy red underwear down to her ankles. Dana kicked them off and I looked at her vagina. It wasn't shaven, but it didn't look that bad. I sunk my head down between her legs and started eating. It tasted awful. All I could think of were the raw clams I had spit out one summer at a clam steam up in Maine. It didn't just taste bad, it smelled bad too. The only way to classify it would be if you walked into a football locker room, opened a locker, stuck your head inside and took a big whiff.

After a minute or two of breathing through my mouth between munches, I lifted my head and started fingering her, hoping that she would settle for that. "Come here," Dana said. She signaled me to bring my head up to her face.

"That's all. You're a tease," she said, then kissed me. "I want to fuck you really bad right now."

I knew this was the girl who would turn me into a man.

We continued making out and I took my T-shirt, pants and boxers off. "Hey, it's been 'awhile' since I've done this," I said, trying to cover up the fact that I was a virgin and would probably be bad in bed.

"You'll be fine," she said.

I didn't have a condom but didn't care. I leaned on top of Dana. Well, here we go, I said to myself and tried to insert. I couldn't get my penis in. I bumped it around her

2

thigh and the walls of her vagina about thirty-four times. Frustrated, she sighed, grabbed my penis, and guided it in. Once inside, I started rapidly humping her like I had seen Ron Jeremy do in one of my father's porns. "Let me ride you, that's the only way I can get off," Dana said.

She finagled her way on top of me and started fingering herself while slamming down on my cock. After a few minutes moans started to get heavier. I got excited and my penis started erupting inside her. "Ah, ah, oh fuck," she gasped.

Then her vagina let out a series of wet farting sounds. She was queefing. Dana sat idle for a minute and than lifted herself off me. Her vigina spewed out my semon like you just took a bite out of a cherry cordial. "Sorry I did it inside you," I said.

"Whatever, that felt so fucking good," she said.

I reached down for my T-shirt and wiped the cum up.

Trashy Girlfriend

For the next few months I continued sleeping with Dana and we started to date. Our relationship quickly got routine. My boyfriend duties consisted of being Dana's personal chauffeur. Everyday I was either taking her to get cigarettes or picking her child up from church daycare. When we weren't doing errands, I was paying for most of the dinner and movie tabs while getting nothing but attitude in return.

One morning Dana called my house at 7:00 A.M. When I answered the phone, I could tell by the slurring of her words that she was drunk. "Can you pick me up at the Mobil Station on Route 28 in Salem?" she said.

Slampig

When I arrived at the gas station, there was Dana sitting on the ground next to the pay phone. She got into my car, and after we pulled out of the station, I could tell she had been blowing coke. She was all geeked out and sniffing up the post-nasal drip every three seconds. I looked over at my little coke fiend girlfriend with curiosity. "So what did you do last night?" I asked.

"Hung out with some friends. Hey, we need to get my daughter at my mother's house. You haven't met my mother yet have you?" she said, all sped up.

"No, not yet. Where does she live?" I replied, falling for her dodge out of my question.

She told me where her mother's place was, then looked over. "My stomach hurts," she said.

"Really? Why is that?" I asked, not even wondering if it was the booze and coke that made her stomach hurt.

"I think I'm pregnant," she said, pulling the visor down and looking up her nose for leftover coke dust.

My mouth dropped. "Pregnant?" I said. "Why do you think that?"

"Because this is how I felt before I had Crystal. Plus I haven't gotten my period yet. We'll talk about it later."

I got a little scared, but didn't want to jump to conclusions, so I blocked the thought of being a baby-daddy from my head.

In a few minutes we drove into a small trailer park community. Dana directed me to the trailer that her mother rented. We got out of the car and walked through a screen door. I looked around and saw that the trailer was as dirty as a frat house on a Sunday morning. There were empty Miller Lite cans all over the place, and about four ashtrays filled with a variety of different cigarette stubs. I looked to my right and saw Dana's daughter, Crystal, sitting by herself under the kitchen table playing with a spatula. She got up and ran over to Dana with open arms. "Mommy," she said.

Dana put her arms out like she was going to hug her, but then picked her up and put her on the couch. "Mom!" Dana yelled.

A weathered, bleach blond-haired lady in tight, stonewashed, 80's jeans and a yellow tank top walked out of the next room. She had a pudgy belly sticking out from under the tank top and reminded me of the crack whores we used to see in the city. Dana's mother took her last cigarette out of a box of Newport Light 100s, and threw the empty box on the kitchen/dining room table. "I thought I heard you," she said in a raspy voice.

Dana's mother looked at me while lighting up her cigarette. "This must be Danny. Nice to finally meet you," she said.

"Actually, my name is James," I said, putting my hand out to shake hers.

She shook my hand, then snickered. "Sorry about that," she said, then gave Dana a wink.

"His nickname's Pile. Um, maybe that's why you thought it was a different name," Dana said, probably trying to cover up her mom's slip.

I sat down next to Dana's daughter and noticed all the cigarette burn holes on the couch. There must have been six to ten. Dana and her mother went into casual talk then Dana's kid started hitting me with the spatula. After a few minutes of them talking about what a dirt bag Dana's father was, the topic in the car came up. "Mom, I think I'm pregnant," Dana said, lighting up one of her Marlboro Lights.

"Well, are you going to keep it?" her mom asked, as if the baby were a stray cat that had shown up on the doorstep.

"I don't know."

"I think you should," her mother said, exhaling a puff of smoke from her mouth. "Yeah, maybe you'll have a boy this time."

If I hadn't lit up a cigarette of my own to calm down, I probably would have had a panic attack.

When it was time to leave, her mother walked us to the door. Outside at my car, I opened the back seat so Dana could put Crystal in. "Let me know what you decide," Dana's mom said in her raspy voice.

On the way to Dana's place, I stopped at CVS to get a pregnancy test. I had to know if I was going to be a baby-daddy or not. In the aisle, I saw that the tests were all in the $25-$30 range. They got us by the balls, I said to myself. On the bottom of the rack I saw that CVS had their own generic test that cost a few dollars less, so I grabbed it.

At Dana's, the first thing I did was take the pregnancy test out of the bag and hand it to her.

"What the fuck is this shit?"

"What?" I said.

"You cheap fuck. You should have gotten EPT," she said.

"It does the same shit! It's not like buying cereal, where Cheerios and TastyOs taste totally different. Just fucking take the test!" I yelled.

She ripped the box open and grabbed the plastic test with her other hand. As she was walking to the bathroom, she threw the empty box on the floor. I quickly picked it up. "Wait, shouldn't we read the directions?"

"I know how to do this," she said, giving me an annoyed look.

I glanced over at her daughter who was getting ready to throw a People Magazine at the cat. "Clearly," I said in a bitchy tone.

"Asshole!" Dana yelled, and walked to the bathroom.

I shook my head. "How many times has she done this?"

A few minutes passed and the bathroom door opened. Dana walked over and threw the test down in front of me on the coffee table. "It will take a few minutes," she said.

She walked to the kitchen table and sorted through the mail. Apparently she waited for her pregnancy results like she was waiting for a tea kettle to boil. I picked up the urine stick and for the next few minutes watched the red dye slowly form a symbol - negative. I jumped off the couch like my mother had surprised me with a new bike. "It's negative, it's negative!" I yelled.

"Is it?" Dana replied skeptically.

"It's negative. That means you're not pregnant! Right?"

"Right," Dana said.

She threw the mail down on the kitchen table. "Do you want to order food or something?" she said.

What I wanted to do was get the fuck out of there and get my head together. I was almost a father! "Um, you know Dana... I really got to go," I said.

I walked over to the door and she stopped me. "Aren't you going to kiss me goodbye?" she asked with her cheek out.

"Sure."

I gave her a peck on the cheek, said goodbye, and walked out the door.

That night I played cards with my friends Rick and Scotty. After a few hands, I told my pregnancy scare story. They toasted their 16-oz. Pabst Blue Ribbons in the air at me. "Congratulations Pile, you're not a father!" Rick said.

"Thank fucking god. Now dump that bitch and move on with your life," Scotty said.

"You think I should?" I said.

"Um, yeah," Rick said. "That girl's bad news."

"Call her up right now. I want to hear you give her the boot," Scotty said.

"Yeah, and put it on speaker phone," Rick said.

I scrolled for her name on the phone and pushed send and then the speaker button. My heart started racing. I had never dumped a girl before. I was always the dumpee not the dumper. "What am I going to say?" I said.

"Oh, fucking Pile. How old are you kid?" Scotty said. "Tell that whore she's going to have to find someone else to raise her kid."

The phone connected. "Hey honey, I was just thinking about you," Dana said.

"Yeah, what were you thinking?" I said.

"I was thinking, maybe we should do something fun tonight. Some of my friends are going to play horseshoes. Interested?"

"Ha, horseshoes. This girl is white trash," Rick said.

I hit Rick. "Um, maybe," I said.

"Pile, don't fall into her trap. Do it!" Scotty said.

"Dana, things just aren't working out. I'm sorry. We need to break up."

There was a long pause. "What? Are you serious? Can we meet and talk about this?" she replied.

I started to feel bad. Maybe I shouldn't be dumping her over the phone. It was a little insensitive. "Okay," I said. "When do you want to mee…"

Scotty grabbed the phone from my hand. "You're fucking through, bitch!" he said and hung up the phone.

"What the fuck, asshole?" I said.

Scotty tossed the phone down on the table. "I probably just saved your life. Come on Pile, the girl's a slampig. You fuck these girls, you don't date them. And for fuck sake, use condoms! The last thing we need is another one of 'you' running around."

He was right. After I fucked Dana, I should have just moved on to the next girl. Continuing to date her would have been the biggest mistake of my life. That statement was proven true when I found out what Dana was doing before I picked her up at the Mobil station. She was blowing lines and getting double teamed by two guys up in Salem. I heard one of their names was Danny.

The First Friday

I enrolled online at a two-year college institute – the kind whose commercials target unemployed people waking up at twelve in the afternoon to watch Maury Povich. I majored in broadcasting and one of our washed-up ex-TV personality teachers recommended improvisation classes. On Monday nights, I had nothing else going on, so I spent a year taking improv.

The first day of classes, we had to introduce ourselves and answer the question, "Why improv?"

None of us told the truth. One girl said, "I just want to meet new people."

In reality she was looking for the attention her boyfriend wasn't giving her. That year she got attention, but a little too much. She was in a scene with the class pervert and they were playing two little kids having a picnic. When she offered him cookies, he replied with "I would rather munch down on your cookies."

After that night, he disappeared from class and our instructor made us sign waivers.

The only honest one in our group was an Indian kid named Paandu. His reason for joining was to improve his American social skills. About five months prior, he had moved to Boston for work. Paandu soon realized that people in Boston can come across as dickheads. After a few weeks, our class's Boston ball-busting began. We gave Paandu the nickname Pandhi, and made many statements like, "Ain't no party like a Paandu party."

He, being proud of his Indian culture, didn't find such phrases as "Party it up like Paandu" at all humorous.

Paandu did want to party it up, though. Because improv was held on Monday night, everyone would hear about my weekend war stories with slampigs. While the rest of the class rolled their eyes as I boasted of tales, such as banging a married chick in the back of a rusty caravan, Paandu listened attentively. Boston girls gave Paandu a huge culture shock. When he told me that it was hard to date them, I wasn't the least bit surprised. Most girls from Boston have a sense of entitlement. The ones who rate 6, on a scale from 1 to 10, act like they're Brenda from 90210. Seriously, it's hard to meet a girl on Match.com, let alone at a night club. That's another reason I went after the pigs.

At the end of most improv classes, Paandu would try to make plans with us for the upcoming weekend. One night he suggested we all go to an event called "The First Friday" at an art museum. The class got quiet and I felt bad, so I took one for the team. "I'll go, man," I said confidently.

"Great, I'll email you later this week with the details."

"Sounds good," I said and went home for the night.

The next few days passed and Friday came around. When I checked MySpace, I saw that I had a comment from Paandu. He wrote that he would be out of work late, so we should meet at the museum. I totally forgot about this Friday thing, but kept my word and commented back, "Cool!"

Museum

That night, I left on the train to go to the museum. When my stop came, it dawned on me that I had no idea what I was about to attend. I brushed off my insecurity and figured it would just be some artsy-fartsy event. An image entered my mind of a bunch of "socialites" eating mini-carrots and reciting some bullshit they heard on NPR about contemporary art. I looked down at my partly zipped hooded sweatshirt with my Tom and Jerry T-shirt under it. "Wait 'till they get a load of me," I said out loud.

I walked through a set of double doors and joined a line of people waiting to buy an admission ticket. When I saw the fifteen dollar cover charge, my mouth dropped. At that time, I was pretty broke. I had just cut back my hours at the coffee shop so that I could take a science course. I started listening to two guys behind me talking bad about Wal-Mart. "Wal-Mart is taking away American jobs by the day. That place should be shut down," said one of them, loud enough the entire line could hear.

I rolled my eyes and looked back at him. He was a hipster wearing a Che Guevara T-shirt, which was probably made in Malaysia by an eight year-old. Then my eyes connected with a hot punk chick that joined the line. With her bleached blonde hair and the rings all over her face, she looked so hot. I loved punk chicks, yet I never thought I was punk enough to get with one. I gave her a small smile and she instantly started eye fucking me. It was serious. It was the eye fucking you get from a college freshman her first week away from home. "Next please," the guy at the counter said.

This broke our connection. I turned my head then walked up to the counter to pay for my ticket. I saw that I could use my college ID to save five dollars. I was psyched: five dollars is two slices of pizza and a Coke. After the transaction I walked away from the booth, passing by the eye-fucking girl. She once again gave me those eyes which begged for me to say something stupid to ignite the first words in a conversation. But because she was in line, I smiled and kept walking.

It was pretty loud in the main room and I thought that it would be impossible to locate Paandu. I took out my cell phone and started scrolling through my contacts looking for the P's. Not paying the slightest attention to my surroundings, I walked head-on into a woman wearing a white cashmere sweater. When I stepped away, I saw that her plastic cup of red wine had splashed all over the sweater. "I'm soooo sorry," I said.

She looked down at the permanent stain. "Look what you did!" she yelled.

I didn't know what to do. "Um, can I buy you another drink?" I offered.

"You should pay for my dry cleaning. In fact, you should buy me a new sweater. This will never come out.

"Once again, sorry lady" I said.

"You ruined my night!"

I started laughing. "Jerk!" she yelled.

I felt bad for the mess I created, but come on, ruined her night? Get a grip.

I walked to the side of the room and found Paandu talking to a short Indian guy in a red silk shirt and gold chain. I tapped Paandu on the shoulder. "Pandhi," I said.

Paandu turned around. "Hey, you made it!"

We shook hands and he introduced me to his friend. "Raja, this is Pile, the guy I told you about, he's a real ladies man."

"I'm not a ladies man. I just hook up with pigs," I said.

They both laughed like I was kidding, but I really wasn't. The last girl I had sex with had acne from her face to her crotch.

When the laughter died down, everything went quiet, so I forced myself to talk. "Hey, I just bumped into this woman and she spilled red wine all over her cashmere sweater. Dumb bitch," I said laughing.

There were about three seconds of silence. "That is really unfortunate for her," Paandu said, not finding it at all amusing.

"Yes it is almost impossible to get a red wine stain out," Raja said.

Before they both labeled me as a total asshole, I changed the topic to our last improv class.

After a few minutes of small talk, Raja excused himself to the bathroom. Paandu looked at me and smiled. "So Pile, are we going to get any trashy chicks tonight?"

I paused for a second. "Trashy chicks? We're at a museum. Trashy chicks come hours from now, at last call in some dive bar when they are slurring their words."

Paandu gave me a confused look. "Well, I'm going to go talk to that girl over there," he said pointing to a pretty blonde in a red dress.

He vanished in front of me like he just took off on a magic carpet. What a real go getter, I said to myself.

It dawned on me that I was now at this event by myself. In this situation there was only one thing for me to do. Drink, and drink heavily.

The First Friday

It was crowded at the makeshift bar. I guessed a lot of people had my same idea. I opened my wallet and overheard a women say, "Good luck, we've been trying to get a drink for an hour."

I looked over at her; she was a pretty brunette in her late thirties. Next to her was a blonde about the same age – chubby, but I would've fucked her. I saw that they were not putting much effort into getting a drink. They were hoping to be seen while standing behind a crowd of people.

Bartending is the exact opposite of everything involving customer service. They are dictators in their glorified retail position, waiting on whomever they want, whenever they want.

I was hard up about the price of admission, but booze is a different story. Like most twenty-somethings, I'd drop half my paycheck (if not all) on a night out on the town, without any buyer's remorse. I smiled at the girls and pulled out a twenty. "Watch the master," I said with a smirk.

I put my twenty-dollar bill up in the air and after five minutes my arm started getting tired. I shook my head in disgust from the shitty service and saw that the two ladies were laughing at me. "How's that going?" the brunette said.

"It's not going good," I said shaking my head.

I just about gave up when the bartender finally looked at me. "What can I get you?" she said.

I was relieved. "I'll have a cranberry and vodka, and whatever my heckling friends would like," I said, pointing at the two ladies.

The brunette and her chubby friend both asked for Zinfandels and gave me a big smile. The bartender came back with our drinks. "Nineteen-fifty," she said.

The brunette took her wallet out of her purse. I put my hand up. "Don't worry about it," I said.

"No, I insist, you're the 'Master' remember?"

"But as Lord and Master, I take care of the people who can't fight for themselves."

I didn't know what the hell I was saying. I think I was trying to flirt. "Oh, now you're a 'Lord and Master,'" the brunette said.

I gave the bartender the twenty. "Keep the change," I said.

"Thanks," the bartender said with an attitude.

We introduced ourselves. The brunette's name was Nancy and the chubby blonde's name was Robin. After introductions we all looked at each other awkwardly and had nothing to say. I again forced myself to talk. "So here we are," I said putting my drink up in the air.

"Yes, here we are," Nancy said.

Then we went back to the silence. I was questioning whether this conversation was worth the twenty that I spent on drinks. I was about to write it up as a loss when an old man, who must have been a hundred years old, walked right through our triangle pushing Nancy and I close together. "An 'excuse me' would be nice there, General Custer," I said.

The girls laughed. "You girls must be the most normal people in here," I said.

"Well, I don't know. You look pretty normal yourself," Nancy said.

"Give me a few minutes. When I get a buzz on, I start talking Klingon."

The girls gave each other a strange look and I decided to save the Star Trek jokes for different chicks.

The DJ changed from jazz to a crappy R&B song that had an easy-to-follow beat. There was a small dance floor set up with some real clown shoes dancing on it. The only one that deserved reproductive rights was a hot Asian lady with red CFM (Come Fuck Me) boots. She looked like she was a hired date for one of the nerd-burgers on the dance floor. I pointed out the group of fools dancing and the girls started laughing. "I want to dance." Nancy said, "Come dance with me."

"You're not getting me out there with that gaggle of dweebs," I said.

I didn't care if I just lost 500 points by not taking Nancy's hand. I wasn't budging. "You probably can't dance," Robin smirked.

"Oh, I can do a mean running man. But those people wanna make me run out of the building," I said, trying to be witty.

Since I chose not to dance, we went into the dreaded what-we-did-for-a-living -talk. Nancy worked for the government and Robin worked for Fidelity. "I work at a coffee shop part-time and go to college part-time," I said with confidence. "So I guess if you add them both up it's a full-time something."

The Captain Cheezmo joke was my way of distracting them from the fact that I was a poor college student.

I started telling the girls that I was going to school for broadcasting. "What do you want to do when you graduate?" Nancy said.

I really had no idea. I was just going to college because everyone else my age was. "Um, you know, broadcast things," I said.

The girls went silent. I felt like an asshole; they probably could tell that I didn't have a direction in life.

Puff Daddy's "Mo' Money, Mo Problems" came out of the speakers and a fat, drunk guy then stumbled by our group tripping over his feet. "I fucking love this song!" The drunken guy slurred then did a spin move and danced his way to the dance floor. We all laughed. "Hey Nancy, you wanted to dance. There you go," I said pointing to him while he was doing something that looked like the twist.

"I think I'll skip the dance with Arty the One Man Party?" Nancy said.

"Who are these people? Did I just enter the Twilight Zone or what?" I said.

Robin sighed and looked at me. "Hey, give these people a break. It's singles night," she said.

In my head I heard one of those record screeching stops and it felt like everybody paused. I looked around at the people and it all made sense. The "eye fucking punk chick," "General Custer," "the dweebs on the dance floor," "Arty the One Man Party" and, oh my god, Paandu. I was at one of those dating events that we all made fun of but secretly wanted to go to. "I thought this was an art event," I said in a defensive tone.

"Do you see any art being displayed? I mean there are a few paintings on the wall but all the galleries are closed. Man, you are in the Twilight Zone!"

I laughed. For an old broad, this Nancy's alright.

After about fifteen minutes of heavily hitting on Nancy, I turned the chubby into a third wheel. Normally, I would have gone after the chubbier one, because it's an easier lay. But Nancy and I seemed to hit it off. There was another lull in the conversation and Robin looked me up and down from my Chuck Taylors to my greasy blonde hair. "Pile, that's an odd name. You can tell you're in college?" she said with a snotty tone.

"How can you tell," I asked.

She rolled her eyes and looked away. "You're hoddie gave it away," she said.

I was insulted and figured these kinds of statements were probably why she was at a singles event to begin with. "Hoodies are the latest trend in fashion," I said.

"Maybe on the Quad," chubby Robin said.

This was the second swipe at me. I was about to make a crack about her pasty make-up, then I hesitated.

"I like hoodies," Nancy said, coming to my defense.

The music then stopped. "We appreciate all of you coming out, but the museum is closing in fifteen minutes," the DJ said.

"So what now?" Nancy said.

"Wanna go to a bar?"

"I'm game," Nancy said.

She was definitely interested in me, but I had to do something with chubby Robin, the third wheel. If we all went to a bar, she would probably shoot me down all night in jealousy. Then I thought of Pandhi. He would lie down on the train tracks for me

"I just need to call my friend. Do you mind if I invite him?"

"I suppose not," chubby Robin said.

I snickered and walked away from the group. It would be perfect; if I could get Paandu on board, the whole scenario would be somewhat comical. And if we didn't get laid, he could at least watch me say something offensive to chubby Robin.

I reached for my phone and saw that there were three missed calls – two from Paandu and the other from my buddy Rick. I called Paandu back and he answered immediately. "Where the hell are you?" he yelled in his Indian accent.

"I have two chicks that want to party," I said.

"It's too late. Raja and I are in a cab with girls. I called you twice to see if you wanted to come."

Slampig

I told Paandu I was sorry and hung up the phone. I walked back to the group. "He already left," I said.

"Aw, too bad, I really wanted to re-live my college years," chubby Robin said.

"Fucking cunt" were the words that ran through my head. I wanted to splash my drink it in her face and watch her make-up run off in hopes she would say, "I'm melting, I'm melting!" Before I did that, I came to my senses. This is the type of bullshit one must go through in order to get laid.

Walking out of the museum we saw "Arty the One Man Party" making out with the hot Asian chick on a bench. I nudged Nancy to look at him. "That could have been you," I said, laughing.

"Oh my god," Nancy said.

"Go for yours, Arty!" I said.

We watched Arty kiss the Asian lady like he was a middle school student in a closet playing seven minutes in heaven. Everyone was getting laid at this singles event. Well, everyone but chubby Robin.

We walked on to the street. At the curb we stopped to get our bearings. "I'm going home," Robin said.

"Just come for a drink," Nancy said.

"I have some work to catch up on in the morning. It's best I get a good night's sleep."

Good riddance. This girl brought nothing to the table. "Aw, don't leave," Nancy said.

I put out my hand, basically pushing her to leave. "Nice meeting you," I said, shaking her hand.

Robin gave Nancy a half hug and kissed her cheek, and then walked off to most likely eat a pint of Ben and Jerry's.

The Crowsnest

Nancy and I were walking, so we picked the first pub we saw. It was called Crowsnest and it was a real a dive, but for me it just meant cheaper drinks. We walked in the door and saw four skeevy guys sitting at the bar. Nancy had a look of disgust on her face. "Is this place okay?" I asked.

There was a long pause. "It's okay," Nancy said. "Just a little more rustic than I'm used too. I'll be back. I'm going to go use the ladies room and wash up."

"Is there even a ladies room?" I said.

"I hope so," Nancy said and walked to the back of the bar.

The bartended approached me. He was a chubby bald guy with camouflage pants and a black T–shirt on. "What's it gonna be kid?" he asked.

I looked at the beers on tap. There was Pabts, Shlitz, and Budweiser. "I'll have a Bud and a White Zinfandel."

"A what? We don't have that kind of shit here," he said.

I looked over to the bathroom to see if Nancy was on her way back. She wasn't, so I had to make a decision. "Do you have any kind of wine here?" I asked.

"What you see is what we got," he said.

"Two Buds than," I said.

The bartender started pouring the Budweiser's when Nancy came back. "I ordered you a Budweiser. Is that okay?"

"Yeah, that's fine," Nancy said.

The bartender finished pouring the beers and put them down in front of us. "Six bucks chief," the bartender said.

21

I gave him eight. He wasn't the type of guy you could stiff on a tip.

Nancy looked at her beer. "I think something's floating in it," she said.

I decided to be a gentleman and trade beers with her. "This is not the ideal place I had in mind," I said.

"It's not that bad a place," she said.

She was obviously lying, the place was horrible. The glass on the pinball machine looked like it had been cracked in a bar fight back in the 70's.

We small talked for awhile about the usual shit, which meant me nodding my head as she was going on-and-on about her life. Nancy was telling me about living in Somerville and having a gay guy for a roommate. "Does he bring dudes back to the house?" I asked.

Nancy rolled her eyes. "He actually has a live-in boyfriend."

"That must be awful," I said.

"At least my roommate and his live-in are 'clean.'"

"Yeah, because they're both gay. Do you ever hear them hook up?"

"All the time. It's like Carnival in there."

When she got to the topic of her cats, I made my move. I leaned over and planted one on her. First kisses aren't like they are in the movies. There is no right moment. You just do it.

A few minutes passed. It was awkward because we had just kissed and everything changed. Plus, one of the skeevy guys kept staring at Nancy. Our glasses had about a quarter of beer in them so a decision had to be made. Were we going to bang, or was I going to have to go home to spank one out to Cougarbait.com.

"So, are you going to introduce me to your cats?" I asked.

She giggled. "I'm sure they would love to meet you," she said, taking antibiotic hand cleaner out of her purse.

I was in. You wouldn't think it, but stupid shit like that works. It's cute and it's asking something without being too obvious and without making her feel too slutty. It was either that, or she just wanted to get out of the Crowsnest before she ended up like Jodie Foster in the Accused.

Nancy's House

The cab ride was about twenty dollars and since she was going to fuck me, I paid for it. This night was killing me financially, but I was about to get laid, so I would worry about my finances in the morning. When we walked into her apartment, I expected to see her gay roommate snuggling with his partner and watching Will and Grace, but thankfully all the lights were off. She turned the lights on. The house was spotless and empty. I whispered, "Is your roommate, I mean, are your roommates here?"

"No they're in the Berkshires," she replied.

"Yes!" I said, like I just won a hand of Black Jack.

She walked over and put her arms around me. "You're very funny," Nancy said, then proceeded to kiss me.

I knew that I was getting ready for some good sex. We kissed over to the couch and I realized that I didn't have a condom. Of course, I thought, the condom curse. You never get laid when you stop at 7-11 to pick up a pack of rubbers before you go out. It's always when the girl is buck naked and asking you to put it in her. Then you have to make the choice. Either go home with blue balls or raw-dog a stranger.

The next few minutes of making out were not enjoyable for me. My head was racing with the whole condom dilemma, but I tried to fake my way through it. It must have worked because she was getting hot. "Do you want to go into my room?" she mumbled.

"I don't have a condom. Do you?" I mumbled back.

She stopped. "No. Maybe my roommate has one."

We stopped kissing and she took my hand and led me into her room. It was so neat and clean, like being in a hotel room. I took a seat on her perfectly made bed. "I'll be back," Nancy said and left the room.

I was really hoping that her gay roommate had some zebra-striped condoms left over from the night his partner brought him to see the Broadway production of Rent.

Nancy came back into the room and tossed a strip of condoms on the bed. They weren't zebra-striped but they were mint-flavored which made me chuckle. Nancy came over to me. "Gay guys always have condoms," she said.

I started to laugh and she grabbed me and stuck her tongue down my throat. Things started to get rough. I took her shirt off. Nancy's stomach was flabby and wrinkly. I didn't care. Nancy unhooked her bra and her breasts dropped two feet down to her stomach. She was a lot older than I thought. Oh well, so I would fuck an oldie. No biggie.

I pulled her pants off and saw that she was wearing granny panties. They were the kind of underwear that your friends would find in your mother's laundry basket, steal, and throw up in a tree. Of course, who was I to talk about other people's underwear? The ones I had on, I found under my futon and hadn't changed in three days.

I proceeded to take off the granny panties and got ready to see her goods. It couldn't be that bad. She was single and didn't have any children. Then I saw it. My mouth dropped. Her beaver was the hairiest beaver that I had ever seen, and my father owned a lot of 70's porn. The dark, brownish-gray, gorilla muff extended up her torso. It almost looked like an upside-down beard. The bottom seemed to cling to her inner thighs like vines on the side of an old brownstone. I didn't know what to do, but Nancy did. She shook her head side to side like a horse who just drank water then grabbed the back of my head. "Take me, take me now!" she said.

Take me? What are we, in the 50's? I don't know what dated her more, the fact that she said "take me," or her ancient vagina.

Nancy had her eyes closed, like she was waiting for a surprise. I put the mint flavored condom on and spread out her legs with my hands. Well here goes nothing, I said to myself. I leaned in and started putting my penis in. I only got the tip in when Nancy screamed. "It hurts, slower," she said, opening her eyes.

It was so tight and dry. I figured with the horse reactions a few seconds earlier, she would be all wet and ready.

I put my hand on my cock and pushed in a few more centimeters. She gasped again. It was so tight. I wondered if this was what it was like to fuck a virgin. When I finally got my whole penis in, I pushed back and forth. Nancy was in pain. "Do you want me to stop?" I asked.

"No, keep going. Don't worry; things should loosen up."

Things did loosen up and I could finally feel her getting wet. It's a weird feeling. Usually the girls I fuck are so wet and loose from the start. I had never felt sandpaper turn into wet cardboard before. I fucked her for a few minutes and I could feel myself about to cum. I slowed down for a few strokes. "I think..."

"Are you going to... you know?" she said.

"Yeah."

"Take it out. Take it out. You can't do it in me."

I had the condom on, but apparently she had the same rule I did. You didn't want it to break and become one of those "the condom broke" cases.

I took my penis out of her hairy vagina, ripped the condom off and threw it on the floor. I was going to introduce this granny to my Generation and dump all over her. I started to stroke my penis and she put her head up. "What are you doing?" she said.

"Cumming," I replied.

Sperm started spraying out of my penis and Nancy jumped up almost kicking me in the face. "Oh my god, stop! I have to get a towel. I have to get a towel."

I didn't stop and dumped it all over her bedspread and onto her pillow case. "Damn it!" Nancy said.

"What?"

Nancy jumped off the bed. "Get up, get up right now!"

She was freaking out and I didn't know why. I got up and stood there in the nude. "I have to get these sheets off before it seeps into the bed."

"Huh?" I said confused.

Nancy ripped the blankets off the bed and threw them onto the chair. She stripped the sheets and put them on the floor. "I may have to put something on this!"

This was ridiculous. We should be cuddling, not doing laundry. Nancy then looked at the pillow case and saw there were some wet spots. She gave one of those bitch sighs that makes the hairs on a man's neck stand up. "I'll be right back."

Nancy left the room and came back with some kind of spray product and started spraying the spots of semen on both the sheet and the pillow case. I was still standing in the nude, just watching the Exxon Valdez-like cleanup.

The spraying finished and Nancy opened her closet door. "Great!" she said.

"What?" I said.

"I don't have another sheet."

"So what? The cum will dry soon. Just put it back on the bed."

Nancy gave me a disgusted look. "Are you serious? We are going to have to sleep on the couches tonight... It's probably better that way."

I couldn't believe this lady and her Martha Stewart sex. It was just a little bit of cum. God, this woman wouldn't want to sleep in my bed. The thing was a dried up sperm bank.

"Just go in the living room. I'll be out there soon."

I grabbed my clothes and walked out to the living room.

A few minutes passed and I figured Nancy was in her room with a chemical suit spraying the place down. A minute later she walked in wearing pajama bottoms and a Harvard sweatshirt. She handed me a pair of sweatpants and a T-shirt that said Club Med. "I borrowed this from my roommate. I'd appreciate it if you'd wear it while sleeping on my couch."

I put on the gym wear. "Did I do something wrong?" I asked.

"I wish you hadn't done that all over my bed. You should have left the condom on or waited for me to get a towel."

"Sorry," I said.

"It's okay. Just go to sleep. You can use the blanket on the couch. I'm going to take a shower."

I lay there thinking about how fucked up she was. I couldn't stand clean freaks. They're usually the first ones to get sick. I kept asking myself, if she was so clean why hadn't she trimmed that bush of hers? The thing was an Amazon jungle. Who knew how many bugs were nesting in that thing?

After her shower, she came out and lay down on the other couch. "Goodnight," she said in a passive-aggressive tone.

I didn't say anything and pretended like I was asleep.

3

Rachael's Mom

On my holiday break between semesters, I went back home to hang out with my buddy Brownie. That night, we were both broke from blowing our money on useless Christmas gifts for our families. So we decided to skip out on the usual hometown hot spots and go straight to Knights of Columbus. It was still early, so there weren't a lot of people there yet.

Brownie and I played pool and he finished our game by bouncing the cue ball over one of my solids, sinking the eight-ball. He grew up with a pool table in his basement and I didn't. So basically, I only got to shoot once.

As soon as the eight-ball rolled down the side of the table to join the rest of Brownie's balls, some kids we went to high school with took their pool sticks off the back wall. They didn't have to wait very long due to my horrific pool skills. One of the kids, Bobby, took his quarters off the ledge and started inserting them into the change slot. "Do you guys want to play teams?" he asked.

"Nah, I'm going to use the rest of my quarters for the juke box," I said.

No one had played any music yet. This was good because I'd be able to hear the songs that I chose. It sucks to drop a few bucks and not hear your selections come up because the old drunks had loaded the jukebox with the music that made them think of the time they ruled the high school parking lot.

Brownie and I walked over to the big, old jukebox on the other side of The Knights. Judging by the selections offered, I was surprised it didn't still have 45's. Scrolling through artists like REO Speedwagon, Kiss, and everyone's stone-washed favorite, Def Leppard, I knew it was going to be tough. The only new CDs were the "Now That's What I Call Music" compilations with the soon-to-be one-hit wonders of the day. While I pushed the right arrow button, scrolling through the rubbish of the seventies and eighties, Brownie made suggestions of what I should play. Every time you put money into a juke box there is always that friend who stands beside you sucking away your quarters by suggesting his own shitty tunes.

A loud group walked into the bar and Brownie took his eyes away from the jukebox to see who it was. "Hey, Scotty's back," Brownie said and walked over to the group. I was excited to see my buddy Scotty, who had been in Afghanistan for the past six months. But I was also happy that I could select the music I wanted to hear without any pressure.

Scotty was a Marine who, from what his father told me, was poking his M-16 through caves looking for the Taliban. I was sure the rest of the night would be filled with crazy military stories. But his stories were not like the ones your heroic grandfather would tell you about WWII while drinking bourbon on Christmas Eve. Scotty's military stories were usually about him and his fellow Jarheads getting in bar fights and hooking up with slampigs.

I made a few quick picks on the box, selecting some Dylan and some Allman Brothers. I started to walk away from the jukebox and out of The Knight's speakers came "Oops I Did It Again" by Britney Spears. I must have hit the wrong button. A huge guy with a mullet and a Gold's Gym tank top who was sitting with his other meathead friend gave me a dirty look. I put my hands up. "It was an accident, I swear," I said, walking away in embarrassment.

I walked over towards the crowd surrounding Scotty and hit him on the shoulder. "What up, kid?" I said.

Brownie gave me a strange look. "Nice song. See, this is what happens when you let this femo pick," he said, pointing at me.

Scotty laughed. "Pile put this on. I'm not surprised," he said.

"It was an accident," I said, laughing.

"Yeah, I'm sure it was an accident, kid."

Holding the center of attention, Scotty said to the group, "Speaking of, before I came here I stopped at this bar, and all these guys were buying me drinks. I figured it was because I was a Marine. The place was great, it's called Rocket."

The group laughed because "Rocket" was a gay bar that everyone used to make fun of. I found it ironic that all my friends were homophobic yet they knew where the local gay bar was. "What do you say, Pile, do you want to check it out?" Brownie said.

"Yeah, yeah, real funny," I said.

Our buddy Lenny, who came in with Scotty, walked over to the group with two Budweisers and handed one to Scotty. "Don't get any ideas. I'm not buying you drinks all night, soldier boy. You're getting the next round," Lenny said.

We shot the shit for a while and all of us dispersed into different groups as more people arrived. Scotty and I sat at the U-shaped bar playing catch-up. "Catch-up" meant him lecturing me about my life. "Seriously, how many years are you going to be in college?" Scotty said.

"Whatever, I almost have my degree."

"Yeah, in fucking broadcasting. Where ya gonna use those skills? Working the drive-through window at Wendy's? The only broadcasting you'll be doing is over the intercom saying, 'Would you like to try a value meal?'"

I was wondering if he was any better than me. Sure, he was a Marine, but he still smoked dope and blew the occasional line of coke. Before Scotty was shipped to Afghanistan, he was in charge of the drug tests at his fort down South. This meant that he always passed.

"All I'm saying, Pile, is when I get back, you're not sleeping on my couch. Wait, who are these chicks? That girl in the green just checked you out."

I looked across from us and there were two ladies whose glory years were probably in the 80's. They both had bleached blonde hair. One was dressed in a fluorescent green short skirt and the other one had on tight jeans and a T-shirt. They were definitely forty-something but still do-able.

"She was checking me out? Really?" I said.

"Yeah, that's a first. We should go over there before anyone else does."

"I don't know, Scotty. They're a little old."

"Are you kidding? You should have seen the old hag I fucked down South, or the hooker I fucked in Yemen. That was fucking bad. Let's go talk to these broads."

Scotty got up and grabbed my shoulder, dragging me towards the older women. When we got to the other side of the bar Scotty didn't even try to be slick. He put out his hand. "Hey girls, we were noticing you from across the bar. I'm Scotty Lavato. This is my friend Pile."

The girl with the florescent green dress looked us both up and down. "Scotty Lavato and Pile. What are you, some kind of cartoon characters?" she said.

Scotty didn't let this faze him. "I'm more of a super-hero, here to rescue you two from boredom."

I rolled my eyes. Scotty's lines were cheesier than mine. "Is this your sidekick?" the girl in the tight jeans asked.

Scotty put his hands up in the air like he surrendered. "Unfortunately," he said.

The girl in green smiled and touched my arm. "Well, don't be too hard on him. He's a cute little sidekick. My name is Holly."

I felt all giddy inside. "I'm Barbara," said the girl in jeans while rolling her eyes over Scotty's body.

I had to hand it to Scotty. He had led us to our lays for the night. They shook our hands. Holly looked me up and down. "Did anyone ever tell you that you look like Clay Aiken?"

"I never noticed that," Scotty said. "Ha, you look like Clay. We should try to get into some Hollywood parties."

"Do you really think Clay Aiken is invited to Hollywood parties?"

"Oh, come on, I love Clay Aiken. He is so adorable and, of course, so are you," Holly said.

I smiled. "Stop, I'm blushing."

"That's what I was hoping for, sweetie," she said, touching my arm again.

This was a done deal. I could probably fuck her in The Knights of Columbus bathroom. Scotty did a smooth maneuver over to Barbara to start dialogue with her. He knew that the girl in green liked me, so by moving on to the other chick, he was being a good wingman.

Holly told me she was a single mother who worked in real estate. I really didn't care, but I had to act interested if I was going to land this broad. Scotty seemed to be doing pretty well himself. Barbara continued to chuckle at Scotty's jokes. She was a cop from one of the nearby towns, which made for great conversation between them because Scotty's family was full of local cops. It was presumed that he would become one once he finished his service with the Marines.

I looked down at my watch and saw that last call would be soon. Scotty and I were going to have to wrap this up and get these ladies somewhere with beds. "What are you two doing after this?" I asked.

"Probably going back to my place. Barbara's sleeping over tonight because she doesn't want to drive back to North Reading."

The scenario couldn't have gotten any better. Scotty knew it, too. "We should have an after-party," Scotty said.

Barbara and Holly looked at each other. "You two can come back with us if you want. I don't have much to drink but…"

"That would be great," I interrupted Holly.

This was awesome. I barely put in any time and now I was going to get laid.

I needed to go to the bathroom before we left so I excused myself and walked over to a small hallway where the men's room was.

There was a long line for the bathroom and I saw that Brownie was at the end of it. There shouldn't have been a long line at the men's room – the women's room maybe, but not the men's. I figured there were some extracurricular activities going on in there. I walked over to Brownie. "What's up with this long-ass line?" I asked.

"Dude, I've been here for five minutes and haven't moved."

"It's the fucking coke heads in there."

Cocaine had either started to become a problem in our area or I had just gotten old enough to notice it. Sure, I've had my experiences with the white lady but when you reach a certain age you're not experimenting anymore. You're just a fucking junkie. It was real sad watching some of my friends deteriorate in front of my eyes. The guy in front of Brownie had his leg shaking. "Come on, man!" he said.

I couldn't take it anymore. "For real. Tell these fucking cokeheads to hurry it up in there!" I yelled to the front of the line.

There were a few laughs. The guy at the front of the line turned and looked at me. It was the guy with the mullet and the Gold's Gym tank top. His eyes started to bulge out of his head and I wondered what his fucking problem was. He slowly walked towards me. I knew I was in trouble. People seemed to get out of his way like he was the high school bully walking down the corridor.

He stood in front of me and as his shadow loomed over my face, I started to tremble. He quickly stuck his hand up and made a fist. I flinched, thinking he was going to hit me. Then he turned his fist into a finger and pointed at me. "Don't you ever, ever, make fun of someone's disability again!"

I looked to the right at Brownie for some support and he shook his shoulders giving me the "You're on your own kid."

I looked back at the guy. "Sorry, I was just making a joke," I said.

The guy gave me a grizzly look and pointed to his still face. "This is me making a joke!" he said. "This is me making a joke!"

I had no idea what he was talking about. I could only hope that he was really making a joke and the steroids had just prevented his face from smiling. "Listen, if I offended you, I'm sorry. I don't want any..."

The bathroom door opened and Mullet Man looked over at the guy coming out. It was another jacked guy. The jacked guy saw what was going on. "Any problems, Jeff?" he asked in a meathead voice.

Mullet Man, or I presumed his real name was Jeff, said to me, "I'm going to go into the bathroom. When I come out, you better not be here."

He walked to the bathroom, said something to his buddy and went in. His buddy then came over to me. "I don't know what you did, but you better go, kid," he said, then walked away.

I was pretty embarrassed. If a beef were to happen, I wasn't sure my friends would do very well against the two coked-up giants. Scotty was a Marine, but he uses machine guns, and I wasn't sure even a machine gun would take these two down. I looked at Brownie. "I better go."

"Probably a good idea," Brownie said.

"I guess we're going back with these girls to one of their houses, so whatever."

"Who?" Brownie asked.

"Over there, the one Scotty's talking to and the other chick in green," I said, pointing to them.

"Oh shit, those aren't girls, those are cougars! Wait a minute."

"What?" I said.

"Is that? No, it can't be."

Holly turned our way, looked over, and smiled. I waved back. "Dude, that's Rachael Stewart's mother," Brownie said.

Rachael Stewart was a freshman when we were seniors. Brownie knew Rachael well, because their mothers were friends. Rachael sometimes came to Brownie's basement parties, where she was always the youngest and most vulnerable girl. "Dude, I can't believe that's Rachael Stewart's mother. She's a fucking MILF," I said.

"Yup, that's her," Brownie said.

"Well, Scotty and I are going back with them to her house. I hope Rachael's not there," I said.

"Let me come? She knows me."

"No fucking way. You'll fuck it up, It's an even number. Get your own MILF."

"Come on, Pile," Brownie pleaded.

"Dude, I know you. If you don't get laid, no one will. You're a prick like that. Plus, if you know her it will reduce my chances of getting laid even more.

"Fine, I see how it is."

"You see how it is? I can't count the number of times you've cock blocked one of us."

The bathroom door opened and the Gold's Gym guy started to walk out.

"Shit," I said.

"Go! If he does anything, I'll bottle him," Brownie said.

I rushed over to the group. "You ready to go?" I asked.

Scotty's beer was empty, but Rachael's mom was still finishing her drink. All I needed was for Rachael's mom to see me thrown through a wall by the cokehead from Gold's Gym. He walked by and I leaned down on the bar, hiding my head and talking to Rachael's mom. Because I was nervous I couldn't think of anything to say. So I asked about her kid, even though I knew her kid was Rachael. "So, um, how old is your child?" I asked.

"She's in high school. Do you want to see a picture of her?"

Women always want to show off their kids' pictures. It's almost sickening.

"Sure," I said, faking it.

She pulled one of those wallet size high school pictures out of her purse. I looked at it. "Cute. Your daughter's cute."

"Thank you, I made her myself."

"I bet you did," I said, rolling my eyes.

"What is that supposed to mean?" Rachael's mom asked with an attitude.

"I was just messing around." I stood back up. "Hey Scotty, look at this picture," I said, trying to get off the topic of me accidentally calling Rachael's mom a slut.

I handed the picture over to him and knew it was a mistake. Scotty grabbed it and said "Shit, I know this girl. Rachael Stewart. She was in my art class. Wow, did she grow."

"That's my daughter," Rachael's mom said. "Wait...you know my daughter?"

I was kicking myself in the ass because I knew this fucked everything up for me. Rachael's mother would feel guilty going after someone her daughter knew and all bets would be off. "Do you know her too?" she said to me.

One of my public relations classes quickly replayed in my mind; I figured I should just come clean. "Um, kind of. She used to hang out at, um, my buddy Brownie's house."

"Adam Brown? I'm friends with his mother. I haven't seen him, well, since he was my daughter's age."

"Well, he's right over there." Then Scotty yelled to Brownie, who was coming out of the men's room hallway. "Brownie, Brownie, come over here."

Now I'm fucked, I said to myself. My lay just vanished.

Brownie walked over like he was just waiting for the right moment to intervene. "Hey, Miss Stewart. How's Rachael?"

Rachael's mom gave Brownie a hug. "Call me Holly. Rachael's good. How's your mother? I can't believe you're old enough to be at The Knights," she said.

"I love this place. Cheap beer." Brownie looked over to me. "Pile, shouldn't you be somewhere where that big guy isn't?"

"I'm trying," I replied.

"Pile almost got his ass kicked by that huge guy," Brownie said, pointing to him.

Scotty looked over at the guy. "What did you do?" he said.

"I insulted the cokeheads," I said, annoyed.

"Pile, you better go. That guy's diesel."

I think Rachael's mom thought we were joking because she went back to talking to Brownie. "We're going back to my house for a few drinks if you want to come."

"Sure," Brownie said.

I was pissed I had just been cock blocked. It was my own fault. I should have never brought up Brownie. Fuck public relations, I said to myself.

"Is Rachael there?" Brownie asked.

She's probably sleeping. She has a field hockey game in the morning."

Now I knew that I was definitely not getting laid.

The Competition

We left The Knights, following the two girls in Scotty's car. The whole way I was screaming at Brownie for fucking up my lay. Scotty didn't feel any sympathy for me. "You should just get out at the next stop sign since you have no one to fuck," Scotty said, laughing.

"No, fuck that. I am going to fuck Rachael's mother tonight."

"Yeah right," Brownie said. "If she's going to fuck anyone it's gonna be me."

"Okay Brownie, she's going to sleep with her friend's kid," I said sarcastically.

We pulled up to a duplex and Scotty parked in the street while Rachael's mom pulled into the driveway. "Hey, Pile, maybe we can wake Rachael up. Then the group wouldn't be an odd number," Brownie said.

"I have a feeling if Rachael wakes up, no one is getting laid."

Rachael's mom lived in the upper level of the duplex. We followed Holly and Barbara up the side stairwell and into a dark apartment. Rachael's mom turned on the lights. "Let's hope my daughter left us something to drink," she said, walking into the kitchen.

"Oh Holly, she has a field hockey game tomorrow," Barbara said.

"I wouldn't put it past her," she yelled from the kitchen.

Rachael's mom came out with five Smirnoff Ices and I grabbed two out of her hands before they dropped. I took one for myself and gave the other to Brownie. "Drink this and go," I whispered to him.

"What did you say?" Barbara asked, wondering what I whispered.

I popped the cap off with my lighter. "I've always wanted to try one of these."

"Fag!" Scotty belted out.

Everyone laughed. "Oh come on. A lot of guys drink these," Rachael's mom said.

"Yeah, at the gay bars," Scotty replied.

I squinted. "That's the second reference to a gay club tonight. Did they use the term 'don't ask, don't tell' as a recruitment tool for you?" I said.

"Not in the Marines, my friend."

Barbara chimed in and touched Scotty's arm. "I love a man in uniform. I would love to see you in it."

From that comment, we knew Scotty's lay was secure; Brownie and I were going to have to duel for ours.

We shot the shit while drinking Smirnoff for about an hour. Scotty told Afghanistan stories and Barbara was eating it up. Rachael's mom was in the middle of Brownie and me so she was getting attention from both sides. I was trying my hardest but I felt I was going to lose the battle. Brownie had something in common with her, so if he ran out of shit to say he could just fall back on topics from the past. Then Rachael's mom stood up to go to the bathroom. This was my shot. I waited a minute and chugged the rest of my Smirnoff. "Does anyone need another drink," I asked.

Everyone's drinks were nearly full, so it was perfect. They all said no, but Brownie said it in a pissed off tone. I winked at him and he gave me the "you're an asshole" look. He knew exactly what I was about to do. I'm sure he's done it a million times.

I walked to the refrigerator and opened the door. Looking in, I saw there were only condiments and alcohol.

It was the refrigerator of a single parent. I heard a flush and when the faucet ran, I grabbed a Smirnoff Ice and remained idle. The faucet turned off and Rachael's mom opened the door and walked out of the bathroom. That's when I went into action, trying to make it look like fate had brought us together in the same room. Rachael's mom walked towards me and smiled. "Well hello there, Mr. Aiken," she said.

I lifted the bottle of Smirnoff up by the bottle cap. "Would you like another drink?" I said seductively.

She walked slowly towards me and our eyes locked. "I would love one," she said.

I started to hand her the drink with my right hand, then put my left on her waist. I leaned in and started kissing her. She kissed me back. I was psyched – I had done it. I had beaten Brownie and she was mine for the night.

A minute later we stopped kissing. I squeezed my arms tight around her, still holding the bottle. "Do you want to give me the tour of your room?" I asked.

"Sure," she said, giggling.

She kissed me quickly then led me into the door off the kitchen.

Rachael's mother turned on the light. Her room had clothes everywhere. There was a pile of what I hoped was clean laundry on top of the bed. "Excuse the mess," she said.

She picked up the pile of clothes and threw them in an empty laundry basket on the floor. Meanwhile, I went to close the door and saw Brownie in the kitchen watching us. He gave me the finger. I stuck out my tongue, shut the door and walked over to Rachael's mom.

We kissed on the bed for a few minutes. I unzipped her dress and started lightly massaging her back. Rachael's mom brought it up a notch and ripped off my T-shirt. My hands slipped under her dress and lifted it over above her head. When the dress got stuck in her bra, I figured I should have taken it off the other way. She laughed as I tried to maneuver it off. After a few seconds of fumbling like an idiot, I finally got it unstuck. "Silly boy," she said, leaning in to kiss me.

She was wearing nothing but underwear and I could see she had a nice body. The only flaw was the old lady stomach – the kind you see at the beach on women wearing swimsuits inappropriate for the Playboy mansion, let alone a forty-year-old.

I stuck my hand under her tight white panties. Thankfully, Rachael's mom was shaved, not like that clean freak from the museum. I started rubbing my palm up and down her clit. "Ahhh," she gasped.

Her vagina flaps were smooth. Rachael's mom pulled her head back as I inserted my index and middle finger. She became instantly wet. I placed my other hand on her stomach and began to rub her clitoris up and down. Rachael's mother put her hand inside her white bra, touching her breast, while she started opening my belt with her other hand. She was either ambidextrous or a slut, because she seemed pretty good at doing two things at once.

With my belt unbuckled and my pants unzipped, my penis seemed to let itself out of the hole in my boxer shorts. She started stroking it slowly. After a dozen strokes, Rachael's mom lifted herself up, forcing my fingers out of her vagina. I wasn't sure if I was hurting her. My fingernails weren't always trimmed. But it wasn't that. Rachael's mom put her mouth on my penis and began blowing me.

The blowjob kind of sucked. It was one of those blowjobs where you want her to stop because you're afraid you'll get bored and go soft. Then you would be the one with sexual dysfunction. Luckily, she stopped before I went impotent. I took off her underwear, then kicked my pants off. I laid her down and got ready to fuck her. "Wait, let me get a condom!" she said.

Rachael's mom leaned over to the bedside table and opened a small drawer. Her ass stuck up in my face. It was nice, probably because she didn't have a desk job. She turned around and handed me a gold-labeled condom. It was a Magnum XL. My penis was big, but not black guy-big. "Who have you been fucking?" I asked.

She didn't find it very amusing, but I did. It's kind of odd when a girl you're going to sleep with has a condom or two in her drawer. You know they're leftover from when she was fucking someone else. In this case, Rachael's mom must have been getting fucked by a guy with a huge cock.

I put the condom on before she took my joke to heart. The thing was loose on me, but would have to do. Rachael's mom lay down and spread her legs. I leaned over her, stuck my penis inside her, and started pumping. There were good and bad things about this loose over-sized condom. The bad thing was that I couldn't feel anything. The good news was that it would prevent me from cumming too quickly, so that I could give Rachael's mom a thumping. And I would need to, considering she was used to having her vagina ripped out by "King Dong Bundy" and his Magnum XL's.

For the next five minutes, I pumped pretty hard and we switched positions to the dog. I grabbed a hold of her ass and started slamming into her. I got sick of looking at the back of her head so I looked down at her ass and my penis going in and out of her vagina. Then I saw that the condom was gone. I had been raw dogging her for the past few minutes. It wasn't broken because the ring wasn't rolled up around the bottom of my penis. It must have fallen have off.

I stopped and Rachael's mother looked back. "Did you cum?" she asked.

"No, the condom fell off." I looked around for a few seconds and couldn't find it on the bed. Then it dawned on me. It was in her vagina. "Hold on," I said.

I opened up the labia and reached in with my fingers. "Ahh," she said as they went in.

The condom was pretty deep inside but I got my fingers on it. It snapped as I pulled it, like when a doctor stretches out a rubber glove. Rachael's mom started laughing hysterically. "That's never happened to me before," she said.

"Well, your Magnum was hanging off. I have a big penis, but I'm not Wilt Chamberlain."

Rachael's mother laughed again. "Who said you had a big penis?"

"Well, maybe not as big as your former lover's, but I've busted out the measuring tape, and my penis is bigger than most of my friends'."

"You guys measure?" she said.

"You bet. Boys are perverts."

I put another one of the Magnums on and we had sex again. We really got into it the second time around. After cumming, I walked out of her room to the bathroom so I could flush the two condoms and clean up. I looked out to the living room and Scotty and Barbara were fucking on the pullout couch. She was riding him facing the other way so they didn't see me. I went into the bathroom and did my thing for a few minutes. When I walked out, Scotty was in front of the door in the dark hallway waiting for me. I jumped back in fright. "You scared the shit out of me," I said.

Scotty walked past me into the bathroom. "Close the door," he whispered.

I shut the door and wondered if Scotty was planning an escape. "Hey, Brownie left in a rage. He's pissed that you stole his lay."

"Fuck him," I said.

"Hey, I heard you banging that broad. Was she hot?"

"Fucking awesome. But all she had were Magnums. One fell off inside her."

"Magnums. Who's she been fucking?"

"That's what I said."

"You better hope that you didn't wake up Rachael."

"She can't be here."

"Yeah, she is. She walked out to the kitchen about a half hour ago. I was getting blown at the time."

"Did she see you?"

"The lights were off. I don't think she saw me. But I'm sure with all the commotion earlier she knew something was up."

I felt bad. It sucks to hear your parents doing it. But it must be worse to hear your mother getting banged by a stranger. Or, in her case, a former schoolmate.

I walked back to Rachael's mother's bedroom and lay down. She was almost asleep. I got under the covers and closed my eyes. That night I went to sleep with a big smile on my face. I had fucked the mother of a girl I knew. Those things actually *do* happen. Growing up, we watch corny movies like American Pie and sometimes kids jokingly say they fucked some else's mom. This night I crossed the lines between fantasy and reality.

The next few days Brownie and Scotty told everyone in my home town. The story spread like the plague. For years, every bar I went to, every late night party

Rachael's Mom

I attended, people would ask if I slept with Rachael Stewart's mom. I felt bad and tried to lie, but when I blushed people put their hands up for a hi-five.

Time passed and for some reason I never ran into Rachael or her mother. One night over beers, Brownie told me that Mrs. Stewart had moved to Philadelphia and Rachael had gone to college in New York, so I didn't have to worry anymore. I then took my knighthood with honor; I was a legend in my town. And for years, when my name came up in a conversation, it was followed by a laugh and someone saying, "Dude, that kid fucked Rachael Stewart's mom. He's the man!

Four Years Later

My buddies and I were at a karaoke bar we go to called Shanghai. As usual, low-lifes were getting their three minutes of fame screaming "Sweet Caroline" into the microphone. I was on my way back from the bathroom when a big guy grabbed my arm. "Dude, you fucked my girlfriend's mother," he said.

I had four beers in me and figured I had probably fucked about forty people's mothers over the past four years. So I had no idea who he was talking about.

"What?" I said.

"Dude, you fucked my girlfriend's mother," he repeated.

Who was this kid? I wondered "Listen, I don't know who you are or who your girlfriend is, let alone her mother. So back off and let me listen to this awful Journey cover in peace."

"Dude, you know who I am, and you know who my girlfriend is."

"My memory is blank. Who are you?"

"I'm Todd Flemming. You remember me, right?"

I scanned my memory bank for the name. It sounded familiar but I couldn't come up with it. Then it hit me. Todd Flemming. I went to high school with him. "Todd Flemming – I know you. You were a few years younger than me, right?"

"Yeah, I moved, but now I'm back. Did you fuck my girlfriend's mother? Her name is Holly, Holly Stewart."

My mouth dropped. This was Rachael's boyfriend and he looked pissed. There was definitely going to be an incident, and my friends were on the other side of the bar. I looked him in the eye. "Man, that shit's just a rumor. She just gave me a ride home one night," I said.

Todd had an angry look on his face. "Don't fucking lie to me, kid."

"Dude, I'm not lying."

I looked over to the other side of the bar in hopes that one of my friends would see the altercation and come to my aid. Then I saw a grown up Rachael Stewart walking my way. I felt like I was on an episode of Jenny Jones. Rachael joined the two of us and looked at me, clearly upset. "Pile, did you sleep with my mother?" she asked.

I stumbled for a second. I couldn't believe what was happening. "Rachael, I swear, it's just a rumor. She gave me a ride home one night because I was too drunk to drive. That's it."

"Are you sure? Pile, I don't care."

I knew the "I don't care, just tell me" game so I continued the lie. "Rachael, I would tell you if I did."

There was a long pause. "Pile, my mother likes younger guys," Rachael said.

"Um, okay," I said. "I never hooked up with her."

Todd looked at Rachael. "Tell him," he said.

I was worried about what she was going to say. Rachael sighed. "My mother just got married."

"Okay. That's great. I'm really happy for her. I'm sure she's with a really great guy," I said.

She smirked. "The guy's twenty-two years old. My step father is younger than I am!"

My mouth dropped. I was about to laugh but bit my tongue because I knew it would result in a sucker punch from Todd Flemming. "Hey, give your mother my best," I said, then walked away.

4

Getting Over Liz

My father remarried and bought a new house. It wasn't just a step-mother that I gained, but a step-sister named Nicole as well. Nicole was eighteen and I was twenty-one, so I was one liquor store run away from us bonding, but it hadn't happened yet. I think the problem was timing. Besides our parents' wedding, the only time we kind of hung out was at her high school graduation party. It was held at the Danvers Yacht Club and I got bombed. I spent most of my time creeping out my step-sister's barely legal friends, by trying to flirt with them. I figured they would think I was cool because I was "older." Apparently a drunk guy in an oversized, unbuttoned flannel, sporting a wife beater and lighting up a cigarette every five minutes wasn't the older guy they were looking for.

I just got back to my apartment in Boston after getting a D on a paper about Nathanial Hawthorne's "The Scarlet Letter." The paper was a huge percentage of my final grade so I was depressed and decided to drown my sorrows with a Natty Ice. It's not that I got a D because I didn't read the book; it's just in my paper, I basically defended the priest and labeled Hester Prynne a Puritan slampig.

I took a Natty out of my fridge and right as I was about to crack it open, the phone rang. I looked at the caller ID and saw it was Rick. Rick had recently dropped out of Plymouth State College because he was involved with a girl back home. When he got back to our hometown, he was happy to be with his girlfriend but unhappy to be living with his parents. I figured he and his girlfriend would soon be moving in together, until I answered the phone.

"Liz broke up with me," Rick whimpered.

"You're shitting me!" I said.

"I'm not. She dumped me last night."

"Why didn't you call me?" I asked.

Rick paused. "I thought it was a bluff. But...oh my god, it was so bad. She wasn't answering my calls all day, so after she got out of work, I went to her house and saw a pimped out Honda Civic parked outside."

"So? She lives in Methuen. There are a million of those Fast and the Furious wannabe's living there. It was probably the neighbor's," I said.

"No man. She didn't answer the door so I went around to her room and looked in the window."

"Oh no," I said, knowing where this was going.

"Then I saw some huge guy with tattoos banging the shit out of her. He was the size of a tank."

"What did you do?"

"What was I supposed to do? He looked like a monster. I guess he's the better man."

I paused for a second. "Let's get one thing straight; no tattooed kid from Methuen, driving a pimped out Honda Civic, is a better man," I said.

"One day and she's already fucking," Rick said.

"Typical chick move. Nothing gets you over the last like the next," I said.

"Seriously, it sucks," Rick said.

"Listen, do you want to come into Boston and drink a few beers tonight? We'll go to a bar and try to get some chicks," I said, hoping to set him up for a rebound.

"No, I'm going fishing with my dad in the morning."

"Fishing? Well, what are you going to do tonight then?"

"Probably stay in. I'm not really in the mood to go out," Rick said.

I had to do something. Rick was one of my best friends and when it came to a break up, he was like me. Soft. "Rick, there's a train that gets into Lawrence at eight-thirty. You can pick me up there," I said.

"You're coming in?" Rick asked.

"Yeah. You're not staying in tonight. We're going out pigging," I said.

"I don't know. I'm not really in the mood."

"Not in the mood? It's the only way to get over Liz. Seriously. My dad and his wife are out of town anyway. We'll bring girls back to their house and if we don't find any pigs, we'll just eat their food."

"What about your step-sister?" Rick said.

"She's a freshman at Fitchburg State. Tonight, she'll probably be getting all liquored up at a frat party."

There was a long pause. "Alright, I'll meet you at eight-thirty," Rick said, caving in.

Home Sweet Home

My train got in and I could see Rick's mother's station wagon from the platform. I walked down the steps and got in the car. "Where's your car?" I asked.

"It's in the shop. It needs new brake lines. The lines were dripping like my tears," Rick said.

"Oh fucking stop it. What the fuck is wrong with you, kid?" I snapped.

"What?" Rick said.

"Dripping like my tears," I said annoyed. "That was the most pathetic thing I've ever heard. It sounded like some shit that would be in some gay ass play."

"Whatever. This night is doomed anyway. How are we gonna get chicks driving a station wagon?"

"What? Who cares what we're driving? It's not like were going up to Hampton Beach to cruise the strip. And even if we were, we're rolling in a Shaggin' Wagon baby!" I said slapping the dashboard.

"I guess," Rick said in a sluggish tone as he pulled out of the parking lot. "Where are we going anyway?'

"I don't know. Let's go to the Shanghai."

"Oh yeah, because the Shanghai is where all the chicks are," Rick said.

"Dude, there are always chicks doing karaoke there," I said.

"Whatever."

I rolled my eyes. I knew the night ahead of us was going to be tough. "You got to get your confidence back and be strong. Like a soldier."

"No chick likes a guy who just got dumped," Rick said. "Girls like soldiers, they don't like wounded soldiers."

"You're right. No chick's gonna want to fuck a guy who has Post Traumatic Stress Disorder from his last relationship. So, I'm giving you from here to the fucking Shanghai to get Liz off your chest. And that's it. After, I don't want to fucking hear it. So go," I said pointing at him.

"Pile, its hard. She was everything to me. And to see her get ravaged by some scumbag... it's just heartbreaking."

"Rick, it just wasn't meant to be. And now that you saw some dirtball fucking her, you know for sure," I said trying to make him feel better.

"Well, I think I got too comfortable. You know? I could have treated her better."

"Dude, fucking stop it. You did nothing wrong. You're so much better off now. Seriously, the girl works at 'The Lobster Bisque.' You weren't gonna marry that broad anyway."

There was a light chuckle out of Rick. "Yeah, I guess you're right. She smokes too. Every time I kissed her it tasted like a Trans Am peeled out in her mouth."

"Seriously, now let's go get some pigs."

Shanghai

We walked into the Shanghai and I was ready to hit on every girl in the bar. Unfortunately, the place was filled mostly with sausage.

Rick ordered two Budweisers and we took our standing positions. "This is such a waste," Rick said.

I sighed. "I thought we were past this, Negative Ned."

"Well, there are no girls here," Rick said.

I scanned the room like the Terminator looking for John Connor. There had to be some signs of life here. "Right there," I said, pointing at a group of girls standing by the bar. "Come on."

I led Rick to their area before he could come up with some excuse not to go over. We stood there in silence for about two minutes. "Is this your plan?" Rick said.

"Um, yeah. So what's up?"

Rick squinted his eyes. "Um, nothing. So anyway."

"Yeah, I can't believe there isn't anyone we know here tonight," I said.

"Yeah. Um, where do you think everyone is?"

"I don't know. Where do you think they are?" I said.

"This conversation is ridiculous," Rick said.

"What do you mean?"

"We're standing here basically pretending to talk. Just so these girls won't think we're creeping on them," Rick said.

He was right. We looked like we were about to commit a bank robbery. After a couple more minutes the girls went to the front of the bar where the karaoke sign-up was. We had just wasted our time fake talking. Rick gave me a dirty look. I had to continue to try to get Rick laid. I would bring him to a whorehouse if I had to. "Let's sit at the bar," I said.

"I don't care."

We sat down and ordered another round. After getting my change from the bartender, I spotted two blondes in their mid-thirties sitting diagonally from us. I leaned my head over to Rick. "I think I see two potentials."

"Where?" Rick asked.

"Right over there. About four-o'clock."

Rick looked over, not even the least bit stealth. "How did we not see these chicks when we came in?" I said.

"They're probably here with their boyfriends," Rick said.

I shook my head. The kid was such a defeatist. "Oh, come on. Let's go find out."

"Okay, fine. But if these chicks don't pan out, I'm leaving for Wendy's. At least there I can get some instant gratification," Rick said.

We walked over to the girls and stood next to the closest blonde. She was pretty hot but as I creepily scanned her down, I saw that her coat was hanging over her left arm as if she were about to leave. It would be a waste of time to stand there waiting for fate to spark a conversation. I was going to have to just go for it. We couldn't just stalk girls all night. If they were going to leave, maybe we could tag along with them to their next destination. I got a little closer and nodded my head. "What's up?" I said.

"Hello," she said, then smiled.

I got a little giddy. I always do when a girl smiles at me. "Where are you from?" I asked.

"Haverhill. How about you?"

"I live in Boston. But grew up around here. This is my buddy Rick."

"I'm Laura. This is my friend Kim," she said, pointing to her friend. Kim had Barbra Streisand-from-the-80s hair and a big nose. Laura was the only hot one and I would rather Rick fuck her than me; he needed it. But I would have to wait a few minutes to pass her off so it didn't look so obvious.

Rick moved over to Kim's area and started talking to her "Are you gonna sing some karaoke?" I asked Laura.

"Probably not," she said.

"Oh, you should," I replied. Not that I gave a fuck; I was just trying to make small talk.

"What song do you think I should sing?"

"I don't know. What song do you want to sing?"

"It would probably be a Journey song."

I cringed. I hate Journey. They are the most overrated band in history and everyone always sings their songs at karaoke. Every time I hear a Journey song I feel as if I was watching some teeny-bop sitcom about heartthrobs and high school. This chick was definitely going to be passed off to Rick. "Maybe you should sing some Sweet Caroline, you know, for the Sox and all," I said, being a dick because it was another generic karaoke song.

"Oh, I love that song. Maybe you should sing it for me," Laura said, rubbing my knee.

Wow, this was an early sign of interest and I could feel the blood stream into my penis. Fuck Rick. He's going to have to fuck Babs tonight. "Only if you sing it with me," I said touching Laura's arm.

"No. But it would be cute to watch you sing it," she said, batting her eyes. "Besides, I only sing in the shower."

Hook, line and sinker, I said to myself. I imagined ramming her from behind in the shower while she belted out "Touching me, touching you."

I looked over at Rick to see how he was doing with Babs; he gave me a ghostly look. He must have been pissed I threw him on the grenade. I mouthed "what" to him. Rick nodded his head to Laura's arm. I looked down and saw that she had a hook for a right arm. My whole body froze up. I was stunned. She had the jacket over her arm to hide the hook. Then she found a moment to introduce the hook as the conversation got stronger. This was probably her test to see if I cared that she had a hook for a right arm. I knew I was going to fail the test, because I was sure as hell not going to fuck a girl with a hook for an arm.

Laura kept asking me questions. When answering, I found myself looking away. I knew if I wasn't carful, my eyes would lock onto that hook of hers. "What's it like to live in the big city?" Laura said.

"Um, it's um, good," I said. My eyes glanced towards the door and I saw a few friends I went to high school with. They must have just showed up. If they saw me macking it to Laura the Hook, I would never hear the end of it. The bartender came over and asked if we needed anything. My beer was almost empty, so this was going to have to be my break. "No, we got to get going," I said.

Rick quickly stood up. I figured that he was just about as interested in Babs as I was interested in The Hook. "Where are you going?" Laura asked.

"We're, um, going to play some pool," I lied.

"Yeah, we're supposed to 'hook-up' with some friends at the Knights of Columbus," Rick said.

I almost broke into laughter.

"Do you want to meet us there?" I asked, knowing we would never be going to the Knights.

"Maybe," Babs said, looking interested in Rick.

"Do you play pool?" I asked Laura. I imagined her hook would keep the cue steady.

"Not really," Laura said, annoyed.

"We'll, maybe I'll see you later," I said.

"Maybe," Laura said, looking away.

I put my hand out to shake hers. When I realized what I was doing, I quickly ran my hand through my hair.

"Bye," I said.

"Yeah, see you," Laura the Hook said in a pissed off voice.

I was an asshole. The ditch was so obvious and shallow. It's pretty sad that I would rather bang a fat chick than a hot chick with a hook.

We walked towards the door and Rick grabbed my arm, giggling. "You should have told Laura to meet us at the VFW. She probably would have found her soulmate there."

"That's fucked up," I said, laughing.

On the way out of the bar we saw our friend Andy. "Pile, buddy. What's up kid?" Andy said.

"Not much. We're gonna hit the road. There's a hot chick over there. She'll probably fuck you," I said.

Andy looked over and laughed. "Who? Captain Hook? She's here all the time looking for victims. Brownie supposedly got a blowjob from her."

"That doesn't surprise me," I said. "I feel bad, though. I started talking to her, and when I saw she had a hook, I bailed. Kind of a dick move, you think?"

Andy smiled. "Hey, you gotta do what you gotta do. That hook's sharp, I wouldn't want that thing scratching my back. She'd give you the Krueger."

I laughed at the Freddy Krueger joke and looked at Rick. "So, what do you say?" I asked.

"Dude, I'm just gonna go back home. This is ridiculous," Rick said.

"Just give me one more bar," I said, giving him the puppy dog eyes.

Rick hesitated. "Where?"

I had to think fast. It was time to try somewhere new. Then it came to me. "Let's go to Peppers," I said.

Rick gave me a weird look. "That place still open?" he said. "I thought they got shut down."

"They did, but they reopened," Andy said.

Peppers is a sports bar that used to serve underage kids. "Okay, I guess we could play darts or something," Rick said.

"That's the spirit. Lets go," I said enthusiastically.

Peppers

It took us about ten minutes to get to Peppers. We pulled into a parking lot full of cars. "This must be the new hot spot," I said.

We walked through the doors and I felt like I was having a flashback to my senior prom. It was packed with kids who looked five to ten years younger than us. "Peppers must be up to their old antics," I said.

"How do they get away with this?" Rick asked.

"Not sure. I guess they make enough money to cover their legal fees and then some."

We ordered a round of Heinekens. Next to us were two young blonde-haired girls. One was tall and had an athletic build. The other was short and plump. Not fat-plump, more like cute-plump. There's a certain glamour to a short plump girl. That is, until she gets a desk job and her ass takes the shape of her rolley chair.

From the look of their grape Kool-Aid-like mixed drinks, they looked so innocent. "What's that?" I asked, pointing to their drinks.

"A Grape Crush," the plumper replied.

"Oh, that must be tasty," I said.

"It is. Would you like a sip?"

I was excited. This marshmallow is going to be my lay for the night, I said to myself. "Sure."

She handed me her glass and I took a sip. It was sweet. It tasted like Dimetapp over ice. "I think I have a new crush," I said smiling at her.

Rick rolled his eyes at my cheesy line as I gave back the drink. "You can take a sip of my beer if you want."

She reached out with her free hand. "I've never tried one of these," she said, grabbing my Heineken.

The instant her beer went back, she scowled like a kid does when their mom forces them to eat broccoli. "Yuck," she said, sticking out her tongue.

This girl definitely wasn't twenty-one; I just hoped she was eighteen. "You get used to it. This is my friend Rick," I said.

"I'm Karen," she said to Rick. "This is my friend Allison."

Rick shook Allison's hand. "And what's your name?" Karen said to me.

"My name is Pile," I said, putting my hand out to shake hers.

I looked down and she passed the no hook test so I lightly squeezed her hand. Our eyes connected. "So, where are you two from?" I asked.

They both looked at each other. "NA," Allison said. "How about you guys?"

"We're from NA too," I said.

"What year were you guys in high school?" Karen asked.

"1998," Rick said.

"Oh, my cousin's grade," Karen said.

"Who's your cousin?" I said.

"Josh Engles."

Rick and I looked at each other. I hated Josh Engles. He was such a douchebag. I was definitely going to try and fuck his plumpy cousin tonight. I just had to make sure this girl wasn't still in high school. "So, do you two go to college?"

"I go to Essex County Community College," Karen said.

"I was going there too, but I took this semester off," Allison added.

Perfect, these girls were stupid and probably whores as well, I thought.

"Do you guys go to college?" Allison said.

"I was going to Plymouth State but took a semester off too. Sometimes it's good to take a break," Rick said to make Allison feel good about her loser decision.

That a boy, Rick. He was coming back. "How about you?" Karen asked me.

"I go to an art school in Boston," I said.

"Oh, you're an artist. O-M-G! So am I," Karen replied.

Yeah right, this girl probably couldn't paint her nails. "I actually go there for broadcasting," I said. "It just has art in its name."

"That's odd. I guess I won't transfer there next year," Karen said.

"If you're looking for a good art school, Mass Art is probably your best bet," I offered.

"I kind of want to go to school for massage therapy," Karen said.

Of course, typical loser dream, I thought.

I talked to Karen for a while and was going crazy. I wasn't sure if it was the instant message acronyms in every sentence or just that she was so damn dumb. Rick seemed to be doing pretty well with Allison so I was stuck. I was there for him, so I would have to put up with dumbing down the English language until I got Karen into bed.

We all seemed to finish our drinks at the same time. I wasn't going to let these girls mooch a free drink out of us, say "B-R-B" and disappear, so I decided to go in for a power play. "I'm throwing an after-party back at my father's house," I said, laughing inside because our after-party would consist of me, Rick and the leftover beers from my father's yearly Christmas party.

The girls looked at each other. "Wait, are there other people coming over? Or is this just a way to get us back to your father's house?" Karen said, pointing at me.

Apparently Karen wasn't as dumb as I thought, or she had been to a few too many of these "after-parties" that led to a bed. "Who said I was inviting you?" I said flirtatiously.

"Oh, playing hard to get?" Karen said.

"Our friends are at the Shanghai tonight. They'll be over later," Rick said, probably scared that my rudeness would blow it. "You're definitely invited."

God, why doesn't he just buy them flowers and chocolates? I wondered.

"So, whatever, are you two in?" I said.

The girls looked at each other. "Sure," Karen said.

"So, do you want to follow us there?"

The girls agreed and we all left out the door.

Dad's House

On the drive to my father's house Rick was acting like we were headed to an eighth grade party to play Spin the Bottle. "Do you have condoms?" Rick said.

"I have two in my wallet."

"Well, I need one."

"When we stop, I'll give you one."

"Should we get more?"

I shook my head. "No time. Plus, we don't need the condom curse."

"Okay, here's the deal. You hook up with Karen since she seems to like you and I'm going to…"

"Just calm down, Rick," I said, cutting him off. "We can't go into hook-up mode just yet. Let's just keep up the bullshit conversation and, well, wait for me to make a move."

"What does that mean? What if Allison wants to, um..."

"Seriously, Rick, just calm down. I know what you're going through right now. Just sit tight and don't tweak these girls out. Okay?"

"Okay," Rick said.

The girls followed us into my father's driveway and got out of the car. "Love the Shaggin' Wagon," Allison said to Rick.

Karen giggled. "I'm surprised you didn't ask us to ride in the back," Karen said, pinching my arm.

Oh my god. Maybe Rick was right and we should just go into hook-up mode as soon as we get in the house.

I unlocked the door and led everyone down to my father's basement. He had his own little man cave set up for himself. Every man needs a man cave – a place with beer, internet porn, World War II paraphernalia and most important, relief from the wife. The only problem with his man cave was that he had to share it with the washer and dryer. So Sunday's laundry day was not a good beat-off day for dad. I opened the mini refrigerator. "Let's see what Daddy Warbuck's has got," I said.

There were two Newcastle Ales, which may be smooth but still a little too dark for the youngins; so I grabbed a few Coors Light out from the back. "Are these okay?" I asked the girls.

"Sure," Allison said.

I gave Rick a Newcastle and the girls their Coors and we all sat on my father's wrap-around couch. Rick and I mostly nodded our heads as the girls went on using their acronyms and bubbly comments. I needed to break these girls up for the both of us. It's usually the hardest part of a double hook-up. "Hey Karen. Do you want me to give you the tour? My dad's house is pretty cool."

It was such a bad line, but it almost always worked. "Um, sure," she said.

We walked upstairs to the kitchen and I put out my hands. "Well, this is the kitchen," I said, thinking I probably shouldn't have led her into the kitchen. Drunk girls love to eat and nothing kills a sex drive like food. I hurried her into the living room before she got curious about what was in the kitchen cabinet. "You look really familiar. Are you sure you don't hang out with my cousin?" Karen asked.

"No, we travel in different packs," I said.

She stopped and put her finger to her chin. "I know you from somewhere. I just can't figure it out."

"Let's figure this mystery out," I said and went in for a kiss.

Yes, it was another cheesy line, but she was young and dumb, and I was older so Karen kissed back, no problem.

We started making out on my father's couch. Karen started breathing heavy, almost like she was panting. She was getting horny and I knew I had to step it up a level. I put my hands up the back of her shirt to take off her bra and she stopped. "I need to check on my friend," she said.

What was this shit? I wondered.

"I'm sure she's fine," I said and went in for another kiss.

"Let me just check," Karen said and stood up.

I rolled my eyes and followed her downstairs. I knew Rick was going to be pissed. I may have moved too fast and blown both our hook-ups. We went down to my father's man cave and Rick and Allison quickly stopped kissing. Rick looked at me and mouthed, "What the fuck, Pile?"

I put my hands up. "I'm sorry dude," I mouthed back.

"What are you up to, girlfriend?" Karen said to Allison.

Rick stood up and gave me a nasty look. "Just being naughty," Allison said.

Karen giggled. "L-M-F-A-O! Me, too!" she exclaimed.

"Always trying to leave me out. Get over here, girl."

Karen walked over and started kissing Allison. My mouth dropped. "Well, this is unexpected," I said.

I nodded my head to have Rick go in for it. His eyes bulged out of his sockets. "Let's wait until we're invited," Rick said.

"Invited?" I said. "Fuck that."

I walked over and started kissing Karen. Rick did the same to Allison. We were all making out at the same time. Allison pulled away from Rick and broke in between my kiss with Karen. Karen stopped kissing us and started kissing Rick. We switched on and off for a few minutes, then Allison stood up. "Lets just all get naked and fuck," she said.

I couldn't believe this; it was like the beginning of a porno. There were rumors that the younger generation didn't give a fuck about anything and were crazy into sex, but I didn't think it was true until now. Allison started taking Karen's shirt and bra off. "Look at these tits," she said, grabbing them.

She started sucking her right nipple. Even with Rick there, it was so hot.

Rick started sucking Karen's other tit then moved up and kissed Karen a few times. Allison moved over to me and I took her shirt and bra off as well. Rick stopped kissing Karen and started undoing Allison's pants. He was a mad dog. I went back to Karen so she wouldn't feel left out and took her pants off as well.

When I got them off, I started fingering her. I looked over to Rick and saw that he was on his knees eating Allison out. She lunged her head and made those pre-orgasmic looks. I felt Karen undo my belt and start stroking my penis. She didn't beat too hard, but she knew what she was doing. Most likely because she had spent her recent high school years jerking guys off on the bleachers at football games.

Allison started gasping. "Okay, I'm ready. I want you to fuck me," she said to Rick.

"Do you have that condom?" Rick said to me.

I grabbed my wallet out of my back pocket and pulled the two connected condoms out. "Oh, I'm on the pill. We don't need those," Allison said.

"I'm on the pill too," Karen said to me.

What about AIDS and STDs? I wondered.

"We should probably use them," I said.

Karen grabbed the condoms out of my hands and threw them behind the couch. "Don't be silly. We're safe. I want you to do me next to Allison," Karen said to me.

The stereotypes about this generation were coming true by the second. They didn't give a fuck about anything. I couldn't believe they were so open to unprotected sex. It must be because they weren't raised with Pedro and the AIDS quilt like my generation.

Karen lay down. "Come on, Pile. I want you to give it to me."

Fuck it, I said to myself.

By this time Rick already had Allison down on the floor with his pants off, ready to insert.

I patted Karen to get up and onto the floor next to Allison, who was just starting to get plowed by Rick. During sex, I had to look down at the girls' bodies because I didn't need to see Rick's hairy chest while I was getting off. It was like watching a porn. There's nothing worse than getting your beat on to a hot chick and then the camera quickly pivots up to some jacked guy humping away. That's when the gay test comes. If you keep your jerk, you're probably a little gay. If you stop and wait till the girl comes back into the scene, you pass the test.

I inserted, fucking Karen like a jack rabbit. "Slow down. This isn't a race. It's good to go slow then build up to a faster speed," Karen said.

Slowing down, I realized that I was getting sex lessons from someone younger than me. I started fucking her around the same speed as Rick. Allison and Karen started kissing each other while Rick and I pounded back and forth. "Oh, my god," came from under the stairs.

My head snapped in the direction of the stairs. It was my step-sister Nicole. She stood there holding a laundry basket with her mouth dropped open. I realized that since Nicole's college was an hour away, she probably came home every weekend to do laundry. "Oh, fuck," I said, pulling my cock out of Karen and standing up. "What are you doing?" I said, shocked.

"What are you doing?" Nicole yelled back.

Then I saw Nicole's eyes gaze down. I followed her eyes and saw that my cock was fully erect. I quickly put my hand over it, then realized it wasn't my cock she was looking at. Karen sat up. "Nicole?" she said.

"What are you doing here?" Karen said.

I went into a panic. They knew each other. "I can't believe this," Nicole said.

She put down the laundry basket and stormed upstairs. "You know my step-sister?" I asked Karen.

"We are good friends with...Wait, that's how I know you," Karen said. "You were that drunk guy hitting on all the girls at Nicole's graduation party."

"O-M-G!" Allison yelled.

5

Never Have I Ever

I moved into an apartment in Allston. Anyone who knows the Boston area knows that Allston is party central. That year in college was the year I started hooking up with random college slampigs on a regular basis. It was so easy. I'd be at a keg party, have a paragraph long conversation with a drunk chick, and then stick my tongue down her throat. I wondered what stopped me from doing this kind of shit in high school. Of course, it was probably for the best. In high school I was so stoned and careless: if I were banging chicks then, I'd probably have three bastard children right now.

The hookups that year mostly involved girls who remain nameless, mainly because I can't remember their names. Even though I don't remember their names, I remember the hookups. Like the Indian girl I argued with on a roof while the party continued downstairs. This somehow led to us making out and me fingering her. Afterwards, when we went back down to the party, she told me not to say anything because her boyfriend was there. I bumped into her going into a room with her boyfriend later that night. She saw me and laughed. "This is my boyfriend," she said, smiling. I shook his hand politely and said to myself, you poor bastard, because he was about to get my sloppy seconds. I was never sure why girls dated in college, since every one of them seemed like a skank.

Ravenwood

It was a Friday night, and I was at my buddy Brad's apartment. Most of our friends were at a Phish show, so Brad and I had nothing to do. We wasted about seven hours playing Tony Hawk and drinking leftover Bud Lights. After Brad flipped out and threw the controller at the TV, we decided it was time to do something productive. When you're in your early twenties, that usually means going out to a bar.

I was already pretty buzzed when we walked into this place called "Ravenwood." We had picked it because we heard a band playing and thought it might be cool. After paying the doorman/bouncer, we realized we had wasted five bucks on a cover band. "At least 'Dead or Alive' and 'Sweet Caroline' get the chicks going," Brad said, optimistically.

I, being the more cynical one, pointed to a few heavy hotties dancing in front of the stage. "What chicks? Those pudgers over there?" I said.

Brad laughed and we walked to the bar to get beers and take a few shots. We had the bartender pour us two shots of Captain Morgan and give us two Heinekens. After paying what a bottle and a six pack would probably cost, we put the two shot glasses up in the air for a cheer. We slugged them back and as the rum hit the back of my throat I could feel it burn like acid. "That wasn't a good idea," I said in a hoarse voice.

Slampig

A few seconds after, the burning was gone, and my voice returned to normal. I looked around the bar looking for chicks who weren't fat. There were no signs of anything under a buck fifty. Ravenwood was filled with heifers so there was no need to walk around and go hunting. If those fatties wanted us, they were going to have to come get us. The shot started to affect me and I began slurring my way through sentences. I trash talked our friend Mike who had dreadlocks and acted like he was a Rastafarian. "Irie, what does that even mean, man?" I said.

Brad couldn't stand the kid either so he added gas to the fire. "The kid's parents own fucking General Electric. He's not Rastafarian, he's a fucking Trustafarian," Brad said.

"I don't know about those 'so called' hippies. Remember the end of that Phish show where that crusty kid said he would fill up our car with his dad's gas card for an eighth of weed?" I said.

"Those kids don't have a clue," Brad said.

We both took our last sips of the Heinekens. "Are you ready for another shot?" Brad asked.

"Negative," I said, making a stop signal with my hand.

"Come on, don't be a fucking girl scout," Brad said.

"Dude, I'm fucking wasted as it is."

"I'll buy," he said with a smile.

I couldn't refuse that. I did wonder what the big deal was. If he wanted another shot, he should just get one for himself. What was up with all this team shit? The bartender served us the same combo. We cheered again and I put it back, chasing the rum with a sip of beer. Thirty seconds later my stomach started rumbling. Then I could feel the booze creep up my throat. I ran to the bathroom and made it to the stall just in time to yak. I threw up a mixture of that acid tasting rum and Heineken all over the toilet. It looked like it was going to be a short night, and we would be back playing Tony Hawk in no time.

Even though I was stumbling back from the bathroom, I felt much better. I saw that Brad was in an altercation with the bartender. Apparently, when I was in the bathroom the bartender had told Brad, "Your buddy's shut off."

For a skinny kid from Westchester County, Brad was a confrontational loud mouth. "Why the fuck is my friend shut off? We're practically sober," he replied back in his deep Westchester accent. The bartender, I guess, was not amused.

"Okay, you're shut off too. Get out of my bar."

"Your bar? You're just some shit-bum, washed-up bartender," Brad yelled.

That's when I got back, wondering why Brad had just called the bartender a shit-bum. Behind us, the bouncer grabbed a hold of our shirts. We resisted and the bouncer pulled our shirts harder. He must have lost his balance because we both fell on top of him. He quickly pushed us off, got on his feet, grabbed us both again, then used all his force to push us out the door.

Outside, the bouncer slammed the door closed. Brad and I just stood in the street looking at each other. "What the fuck just happened?" I asked him.

"I'm not sure. They think you're drunk," Brad replied.

"I am. I just puked up battery acid in the bathroom," I said.

"Yeah, but being drunk is the point of being at a bar. If I wanted to be sober I would hang out at fucking Starbucks," he said.

"Fuck it. Let's go back to your place."

"No, we're going back in there to show that pussy who's boss."

I didn't want to go back in, but Brad walked through the door so I had to follow. Inside the bouncer was talking to the bartender most likely about what just happened. "You want some of this, you fucking faggot?" Brad yelled to the bouncer.

The bouncer charged at us, and I saw everything in slow motion. Brad threw a punch and missed. The bouncer grabbed both of our shirts and pushed us outside again. "You stay the fuck out of here!" he yelled.

He threw us into the side of a white Geo Prizm parked out front. We hit the car and fell to the ground. The bouncer turned back around. "Fuckin' punks," he yelled and closed the door. We hadn't exactly met our match, but we met an embarrassing situation. We got up and thought it best to leave.

Fascism

Barfing and getting thrown into a Geo Prizm pretty much sobered me up. Brad was yelling about going back with a bat. I just laughed at him. It was over, and even though we sometimes talked like we were tough we certainly weren't. We walked by two girls talking in front of an apartment complex and the pretty one stopped us. "Do either of you have an extra cigarette?"

Brad looked down at the lit Newport Light in his hand. "Well, I guess lying wouldn't do me any good," he said, smiling.

Living in the city and smoking butts was worse than smoking in high school. Every time you had a butt lit, some homeless guy would come out of an alley and say, "Hey, my man, can you spare a smoke?"

This girl wasn't homeless though. She was a cute brunette with a nice body. Her friend, however, was fat. "If you don't have enough, it's okay. We're on our way to 7-Eleven," she said.

Brad took a pack out of his pocket. "Nah, I was just fucking around," he said handing her a smoke.

She took it and looked at the brand. "Eww, Newports. I can't believe I just met someone my age that smokes Newports," she said.

"What do you smoke?" I asked.

Brad interrupted. "Let me guess. Parliaments?"

"Nope...."

"How about Marlboro Lights?" I said.

"Close."

Brad put his head up. "It can't be Marlboro Reds. Can it?"

"Camel Lights."

"I should have known," Brad said, lighting the girl's cigarette.

"Thanks," she said, blowing out her first drag.

"What are you guys doing tonight?" her fat friend asked.

"Not sure," I said. "We just left a bar."

"Yeah, more like got thrown out," Brad mumbled.

"What are you two doing after 7-Eleven?" I asked.

"We're at my friend's party. It's a house party if you want to go," the fatty said.

I looked at Brad in hopes that he felt the same enthusiasm I did at finding a party.

"Yeah, we'll check it out. Should we wait for you to come back or do you want..."

"Just go up there. We'll be back soon," the fat girl belched.

"What number is it?" Brad said.

The fat girl urged us to follow her into a set of doors, then rang the buzzer just inside. A few seconds later someone from upstairs buzzed the door, unlocking it. "See, it's cool, just go up."

"Um, thanks," I said, wondering why the fatty was so eager for us to go to the party. I figured she must be man-hungry. She probably had a better shot of hooking up if she increased the number of men up there.

The brunette smiled at Brad. "We'll be back soon. Don't worry about it – my friend is cool."

I saw she liked Brad which meant I would have to hook up with the fatty. I was a good friend, willing to jump on the grenade if the occasion arose. We thanked the girls and they left. Brad and I walked into the apartment building and started up the stairs.

"Dude, did she tell you what apartment the party was in?" I said.

"Nah, did you see which button she buzzed?"

She had rung the buzzer right in front of me, but as usual, I hadn't been paying attention.

"Fuck," I said, slapping my head.

"It's okay," Brad said. "We'll just listen in at the doors for the party."

We walked up a few flights of stairs and heard a commotion coming from apartment 32. "This must be the place," I said. "Knock on the door."

"You knock."

"No, you knock."

Brad gave me a fucked up look. "Like it matters who knocks? Both of us are going to be out here when they open the door," he said.

"Okay, then you knock," I said in a defensive tone.

"Fucking pussy!" Brad yelled and began to knock.

No one answered so Brad knocked again louder. A few seconds later the door swung open and standing in front of us was a huge skinhead. He was your stereotypical skinhead in his black boots, rolled up jeans, a chain link wallet and bomber jacket. He was also built like a Mack truck and just looking at him made my heart stop. "Can I help you boys with something?" he said.

We didn't say anything and he squinted his eyebrows. All we had to say was, "I think we have the wrong apartment." But for some retarded reason I said in a wimpy voice, "We heard there was a party and thought, and well you know?"

He paused for a second. "Um, I don't know, kid. You thought what?"

I could feel my face turning red and looked down at my feet.

"Um, um, um," I mumbled.

Another skinhead came over who looked like Vin Diesel. "What's going on?" he asked.

"We got some party crashers."

"Party crashers?" the Vin Diesel guy said.

I lifted my head. "I'm sorry, we were..."

The skinhead cut me off. "You guys hear a party going on and you think you can just drop by? Well, it's not cool man. It's not cool!" he said.

"A girl told us we could stop..."

The skinhead slammed the door in our faces with a bang. Brad and I jumped a few inches off the ground. Brad looked at me. "First the bouncer, now this. We are destined to get our asses kicked tonight," he said.

"Do you want to go back with your bat?" I joked.

"Fuck that shit," Brad said and we headed back downstairs.

Party

Walking out of the apartment building, we saw the two girls on their way back from 7-Eleven. "Hey, why are you two leaving?" the fat girl said.

"Um, your host wasn't too friendly," Brad replied.

"That doesn't sound like Janice," the pretty girl said. "Did you tell her we said you should come by?"

"Some big, bald guy told us that it wasn't cool and slammed the door in our faces," I said.

"Big, bald guy is an understatement. Some skinhead told us that it wasn't cool," Brad chimed in.

The girls stopped for a second and laughed. "Oh you guys went to the wrong apartment. The skinheads live on the floor below. Those guys are assholes. You're lucky you didn't get beat up," the hot chick said.

"I know," I chuckled.

"I'm Ann, by the way," the hot girl said.

The fatty gave me a smile. "I'm Jenny. Let's go to the right party and get our drink on."

I was sure she wanted to get more than her drink on. There must be some appetizers there as well.

We walked back up the stairs, passing the skins' door. "Wanna try a second time?" Brad said to me.

"Nah, look what happened when we went back in the bar."

The four of us continued to the right apartment a floor above. Just inside was a pretty boy with gelled hair and a collar that looked like it was held up with starch. "Annie Girl!" he shouted and gave her a hug.

They started small-talking. Brad looked upset; he had just lost his lay to some "pretty boy." Jenny took over and led us into the kitchen where a number of kids used blue Solo cups to scoop red liquid out of a plastic trash barrel. Jenny stopped a girl and introduced us. "This is Janice, the host of the party."

"Hope you boys like Jungle Juice," Janice said, handing us two Solo cups.

I had never had Jungle Juice before, but I'd heard it knocks you on your ass. I was worried that I might puke again, but free booze was free booze. We dipped our cups into the trash can. A small Asian guy walked in the kitchen. "Hello my dear!" Jenny said to him.

They got into a long conversation and Brad and I were both left to fend for ourselves. That was fine by me. I would rather not have fat Jenny hanging on to me all night.

On the walk out of the kitchen, Janice stopped us. "Did you guys get a lei yet?" she asked.

I thought she said, "Did you guys get laid yet?"

"No, not yet.," Brad said.

I looked over at him with a strange look. Janice walked over to the refrigerator and took two Hawaiian leis off the top. She put them around our necks. How long am I going to have to wear this stupid thing before I can take it off without offending Janice? I hate those plastic Hawaiian flower things. What's the point? They look stupid and they are obviously not going to help any guy get laid. If that were the case you would see of the clubs full of meatheads in pink shirts wearing them around their necks.

We walked down the hallway past college students drinking and having a good time. Brad took his lei off and threw it on the floor. Apparently, he felt the same way I did. I threw mine on the floor as well. We walked to the end of the hall and entered a bedroom with a group of girls sitting around. There were six girls in the room and they all were pretty hot. One girl was punk and looked out of place in this party full of Ivy Leaguers. Because they were all sitting in a circle, I thought they were smoking pot and prepared to mooch a few hits. "What's going on in here?" I said like I was someone's upset father.

"Hey, we're playing 'Never Have I Ever.' Wanna play?" one of the girls on the bed asked.

I didn't hang out at a lot of girls' slumber parties growing up, so I had never heard of the game. "Is it a drinking game?" Brad asked.

"We're playing the drinking version," one girl said.

"Then sign us up," I replied.

A drinking game is the best way to get to know people. Especially girls.

"Come sit," said the girl on the bed.

There was room on the bed between two girls. Brad seemed to leap over a couple girls sitting in chairs to get to the spot before me. I stood for a second because there was nowhere to sit. "Should I get a chair from the next room?" I asked.

The punk chick moved over a few inches on a large circular wicker papasan chair. "You can share with me. But no funny business! I have a boyfriend," she said with a smile.

"Don't you worry, I'm a gentleman."

"Yeah, he has a boyfriend too. That's why he said he's a gentleman," Brad said, making a bad joke.

"Are you the butch and he's the bitch?" the punk chick asked him.

Everyone laughed. I liked this girl already. First off, I had an attraction for punk chicks and second I loved a good ball-buster.

The girl on the bed explained the game to us. It was simple: you tell the group something personal or embarrassing that you've done by saying, "Never have I ever [personal thing]." Then the others in the group who have done that same personal thing take a sip of their drink.

For instance, if someone said, "Never have I ever been to New York City," everyone who had been to New York would drink. It's simple. What I soon learned was that the game could get dirty quickly, which is a good way to get girls horny.

The girl in the chair next to the bed started. "Never have I ever been on a blind date."

All of the girls sipped their drinks. I wasn't sure if MySpace hook-ups counted as blind dates so I kept my cup idle.

"Never have I ever smoked a cigarette," the girl on the bed said.

This is one where we all took a sip. Now it was Brad's turn and I was curious to hear what he was going to say. "Never have I ever done cocaine."

Brad was a fucking asshole because he knew I had done it on more than one occasion. As I took a sip from my cup, I saw the punk girl lift her cup as well. We both laughed. "Well, now we know who the druggies in the room are," one of the girls said.

The girl next to Brad laughed. "Someone frisk those two on the way out. They may be stealing to get drug money," she said.

The punk girl put her hand up. "It was only once, and I was drunk," she said.

"I guess the DARE program didn't teach you very much," I said.

"What about you?" she replied.

I filtered out the many late night blow parties and came up with a story from high school. "In high school I was in a Winnebago before an Aerosmith concert, pre-gaming with a bunch of 70's trash," I said.

"I see," she said.

"Yeah, the best was the guy in front of me who was saying I shouldn't mess around with it as he was doing it himself. Then what does he do? He passes me a line to blow, from off of the Steve Miller Band Greatest Hits CD."

The game continued and the topics ranged from throwing up on a roller coaster to butt sex in the back of a car. This game was great. After one of the girls left, I was worried the game would come to an end. I had a real connection with the punk girl and from what I could tell, her boyfriend wasn't at the party. So I said to myself, "the hell with it."

On my turn, I went for one of the cheesiest power plays I'd ever attempted. I paused for a second. "Never have I ever kissed someone whose name I don't know," I said.

Then I leaned over and kissed her. I caught her off guard but she didn't hesitate when I stuck my tongue down her throat, kissing me back. "Whooo," the girl on the bed said. We stopped kissing and both took a sip from our cups. It was so cheesy. I could tell Brad knew it as well when he shook his head smiling.

The game broke up after a few more turns and a few girls left to get more drinks. It was now Brad and me and the two girls in the room. My punk chick told me her name was Sarah and that she lived in the building.

"My, um, roommate has people over but I don't like some of my roommate's friends so I came up here," she said.

"Maybe we can go back there later?" I asked.

She hesitated. "Um, maybe."

That didn't sound very promising. I was going to have to do all my business with her at the party, which meant public displays of affection. It's an embarrassing and risky move but it's one I'd played many times at keg parties and concerts. After some more small talk I went in for another kiss. We started making out and I could hear

Brad and the other girl's awkward small talk. It was funny to hear them try to pretend there wasn't a couple in the room going at it. He should have used that moment to kiss the girl on the bed, but when it comes to chicks, he's soft.

After a few minutes I whispered in her ear, "Let's go down to your place."

"We can't. I told you there's people down there."

"Can we go anywhere else?" I asked quietly.

She stopped for a second to think. "I think I know a place," she said. We got up to leave. "We'll be back," I said to Brad. As the girl beside him said goodbye to Sarah, I mouthed silently, "Hook up with that chick."

"I'm trying," Brad mouthed back.

"You're not trying hard enough," I quietly replied.

The Laundry Room

Sarah led me out of the apartment to the stairway. I followed her all the way down to the basement, not asking any questions. That's lesson one when trying to hook up with a chick: don't ask too many questions. You don't want to freak her out and have her change her mind. We walked into the laundry room. Sarah put her hands up. "It's kind of trashy but..."

I cut her off. "It's somewhere, right?" I said, then proceeded to kiss her.

We were going at each other pretty rough. That's what I loved about these punk chicks. They were wild. I put my hands up the back of her shirt to unhook her bra. There was no hook and I knew she could sense me struggling for a few seconds. "It's in the front," she said.

"Oh, okay."

I reached up the front of her shirt and pushed in on the plastic strap, unhooking the bra. I spread my hands over her boobs. They couldn't be anymore perfect. I wanted to suck the firm and perky C cups, but it's not really something you do standing up.

After a few minutes it was time to take it to the next level. "Will you go down on me?" I asked quietly.

Asking for a blowjob is always awkward, unless you knew she was a slampig from the beginning. Then I would have pulled away from the kiss, groaned and said, "Suck my cock." As if it were an order.

She looked up at me. "Only if you go down on me."

I thought about it for a second. It's hard to agree to go down on a girl without first seeing the goods. But this chick was young and hot. I was sure her box wasn't hairy and slimy like some of the pigs I'd been with.

I lifted her up on the dryer. Unbuttoning and unzipping her tight punk jeans, I knew this was going to be difficult. I lifted her butt, which helped me pull her pants and underwear down to her knees. I knew I wouldn't be down there long, so I didn't make a big project out of it by taking off her big leather boots. Looking down at her vagina, I liked what I saw. It was shaved and well molded. It was nice, not like the banged up vaginas I was used to back home. The girls from back home fuck up their vaginas by getting fat and lazy, and subjecting their boxes to overuse. This girl's was perfect. I knelt, stuck my head under her legs, and went to town on the bare, gentle muff. It tasted so good. Almost like lemonade on the hottest day of summer.

After a few minutes of pure enjoyment I wondered if I was the only one enjoying it. I didn't hear any heavy breathing or moans coming from her. I lifted my head. "Does this feel good?" I asked.

"Yeah, why?" she replied.

"You're not doing anything."

"Oh, sorry. No, it feels great!" she said giving the Tony the Tiger arm motion.

I went at it again and she started to make fun of me. "'Oh yeah, this is hot. Oh, right there.' Is that what you wanted?" she said, making fun of me.

I popped up from between her legs. "Okay, very funny," I said. "My turn."

"Ah, just when it was getting good," she said as she scooted off the dryer.

Sarah pulled her pants and underwear up at the same time. When she was done zipping and adjusting, she got down on her knees and undid my belt. "Let's see what we have here," she said.

She pulled my pants and boxers down to my ankles and my hard cock bobbed up and down like a spring. "You have a nice penis," she said.

"Enough of the jokes," I said.

"No, it's nice. Not too big and not too small."

"Is that a Goldilocks and the Three Bears reference?"

She laughed. "We could make a porn," she said.

"Yeah, Goldilocks and the three cocks," I said, laughing.

"Three cocks are a little overwhelming. Well, let's see if it tastes 'just right,'" she said, grabbing my penis. As she started sucking, I put my hand on the back of her head. It felt really good but probably wouldn't last long: I was already on the verge of cumming.

Then I heard someone come in the room. "Son of a bitch!" a man's voice yelled.

Sarah flew off me back into the dryer and I looked over, instantly pulling my pants up. It was the huge skinhead from earlier. "God damn it Sarah! What the fuck is this shit?"

"Brett, I'm, I'm..."

"You leave our party to do this? This is the second time I've found you down here with anotha guy, you fuckin whore."

"Oh yeah, 'our' party. Those are all your friends. I hate those assholes," Sarah yelled.

Suddenly, everything became clear. She wasn't punk; she was a slutty skinhead chick who lived with her boyfriend. Regardless of the details, I was a dead man.

Brett the skinhead was in a rage. He started screaming at Sarah, who screamed right back. I started to casually walk by them, zipping up my pants on the way to the door as if the whole thing didn't concern me. "You're not going anywhere!" the skinhead yelled.

He grabbed me by my neck and threw me across the room into a washing machine. I slammed into it with a thud and fell on my ass. As he moved towards me, I jumped up to run past him - not the best of ideas. He threw a punch at my right eye that landed harder than Drago's in Rocky 4. I flew back and landed on the ground, nearly unconscious. "You're the guy who tried to crash my party," he yelled.

Then I felt a steel toe boot kick me in the stomach; I knew I would be seeing a white light soon.

I heard Sarah yelling repeatedly, "I fucking hate you! I fucking hate you!"

My left, not-swelling eye opened in time to see Sarah jump on his back and start punching his head. I knew it was now or never. I had to get up and get the fuck out of that laundry room. A sudden rush of adrenaline came over me and I booked it past them. The skinhead turned, and with Sarah still on him, started to come after me. She clawed her nails into his bald head and he started to scream. "Go!" she yelled at me.

Running up the stairs, I thought about Brad. If the skinhead saw him in the building and associated him with me, he'd be dead. I also thought about Sarah. Even though she was a slutty skinhead chick, she had saved me. Who would save her? I saw a fire alarm in the hallway and pulled the lever. A loud siren went off and I ran out the door. I dashed around the corner to watch everyone evacuate the building. A minute or two later I saw Brad with a bunch of girls from upstairs and ran over to him. "Yo, we gotta go!"

"What the fuck happened to your eye?" Brad said.

"I'll tell you later. Let's just get the fuck out of here."

The girls next to us looked at me like I had just torched the building. Then Sarah and Brett came out screaming at each other. I grabbed Brad and pulled him away. On our walk around the block I saw some fire trucks drive past us and then a few police cars. I had caused a major scene and hopefully saved Sarah. But I didn't stick around long enough to see.

6

Threesome?

It was my last semester and I needed an internship to graduate, so I signed up for one in Italy. I lived and worked with these Italian artists on the Riviera. When it comes to work, Italians are pretty lax. They never gave me a set schedule so every morning was a mystery. I don't think Italians have set schedules for anything. There was always a bar, a café, or a conversation to delay whatever work needed doing. Each morning when I woke up, they told me if they needed me or not. To be working in Italy without a set schedule was kind of a pain for someone who wants to explore the world. But I was probably better off that way. Otherwise, if I had three to four days of scheduled vacation, I would have been on the first train to Amsterdam to smoke dope, eat space cakes, and bang hookers.

On one of my mornings off, I sat back on a metal lawn chair looking out at the Riviera and pondered how I would spend my day. I narrowed it down to two possibilities: either continue reading Stephen King's *The Stand* or take a day trip. A few days earlier I'd had dinner with some Romanian artists who told me about a famous casino in Monaco named the Monte-Carlo. I love blackjack so I put *The Stand* away, put some gel in my hair, and left the house.

I began to walk down the small mountain the Italian artists lived on. As pretty as the scenery was, the walk down sucked balls. The road curved in a spiral down the mountain and had no sidewalk. That meant when you walked around a turn you had to look out for oncoming cars. Any second, you could be whipped by one of those smart cars driving 50 miles an hour. When I first arrived in Italy, the artists offered me a scooter to ride around on. At first I pictured myself buzzing through small villages made of stone with a beautiful signorina holding onto my back. That dream faded quickly after a few minutes of watching those Italians drive. They are crazier than drivers from Jersey. Plus I have severe ADD. I'd probably be driving down a beach boardwalk, spot a topless chick sunbathing and plow into a telephone pole.

When I got to the bottom of the mountain, I walked into the train station and looked at the schedules. I had about a half hour to kill before my train to Monaco would arrive. This was good; I could get some coffee and biscotti before my journey to the casino. I walked over to the ticket booth. "Salva, un biglietto treno Monaco," I said to an old timer working the booth.

I wasn't sure that was the right order of words, but he knew what I was talking about. The ticket guy asked me something which I figured meant one way, or round trip. I spun my finger around in a circle indicating that I wanted a round trip ticket. He pushed a few buttons and a price came up. I gave him a twenty and he gave me some coins as change.

The guy in the booth handed me my ticket. "Grazie," I said, thanking him in Italian.

"Prego," he replied.

I walked into the café and saw a few Italians drinking wine. I was amazed. It wasn't even eleven o'clock and these people were already boozing. The bartender was in his late 20s and was talking to a middle-aged man. I walked over and stood there for about three minutes until the bartender noticed me. The service in Europe is as bad as going to a Kentucky Fried Chicken in Alabama. You wait an hour just for them to look at you. Then after you order, it takes an hour just to get the wrong thing.

The bartender said something in Italian which was probably, "Can I help you?"

I nodded my head. "Un café freddo," I said, meaning coffee cold.

The bartender laughed. "You want ice coffee?" he said, knowing I was American.

"Si," I said.

He started going to work on the espresso machine. "I like Dunkin Donuts," he said.

"Me too," I replied.

A minute later the bartender poured two espresso shots into a martini mixer full of ice and took out a carton of milk. "Latte?" he asked.

"Si," I said.

He poured the milk into the espresso up to the top of the mixer snifter. "Grazie," I said.

"Prego."

The bartender leaned in over the counter. "You go to college?"

"Sì," I said.

The bartender smiled. "I want to go to American college. Pretty girls. Is it like the movie American Pie? Where you just have fun with them?" he asked.

90

"I thought it was like that over here," I said, recalling the movie Euro Trip.

"No, no, no. Not here," he said.

I smiled. "Not in America either. That's the movies. If you want to have fun with a girl you don't know, the girl has to be grande," I said putting my arms out to symbolize a fat chick.

"In Italia too," he said.

It only took a few sips to finish my cold coffee. It was ironic to me that the Italians spend hours a day in coffee shops drinking small cups of espresso. And we Americans buy huge coffees then dart out the door to go nowhere. I said "ciao" to the bartender and walked out of the café and to the train track.

Monaco

Some time passed and I got on the train and sat in one of the small rooms with a lady from England. We spoke for a while about tourism until her stop came. I really enjoyed taking trains in Europe because you met people from around the world. The train arrived in Monaco an hour later. I got off, and followed a long maze of corridors to an exit. I thought that the Monte Carlo casino would be just outside the train station, but I was wrong. A guy in a suit walked by me and I stopped him to ask where the casino was. He told me that I had to take some numbered bus. I got worried so I wrote the number down on my hand; that way I wouldn't be lost later.

I got off the bus and there it was, the Monte Carlo casino.

I looked up at the luxurious palace. "I'm going to lose my shirt here," I said aloud.

Then I looked down at my Converse All-stars. "No I'm not. I'm not even going to be allowed through the doors."

I walked by a parked Ferrari and Porsche and then entered. There was a lady behind the glass at check-in. I gave her ten Euro to enter the casino, and she showed me how to get into the main part. It dawned on me that even though there were luxury cars outside, this casino was like most American casinos. They aren't interested in your attire, just your money.

The main gambling area was small, but beautiful. It wasn't busy and I wondered if there were more rooms with other tables. I walked over to a connecting room, which was even more beautiful. I tried to enter and a security guard sprang up and blocked me with his arm. "Fermé," he said in French, meaning "closed."

I peered my head over his arm and looked inside. The area was for high rollers but it looked more like a museum. The security guard looked at my curious face. "No James Bond today," he said smiling.

I laughed at his joke and asked where the ATM was. He pointed me into another room where the slots were. I thanked him in French and walked over, prepared to be raped by ATM fees.

In Europe, I was always skeptical about using the ATMs and worried that there was a Gypsy in the back writing down my bank account information. This one charged me five Euro which wasn't bad. The previous day I'd been charged ten and went apeshit. But what are you going to do? The ball is in their court. I went back into the main room and cashed two-hundred Euro into chips.

"Good luck," the fat man behind the counter said.

The grin on his face said, "Thanks for the money, sucker!"

Threesome?

I figured I should go to the bathroom before hitting the blackjack table. Better to win or lose my money all in one swoop instead of breaking it up into small increments. Like a professional gambler, I put my chips in my jeans pocket and walked into the bathroom. I peed, and then went over to the sink to wash my hands. The casino had a hand dryer which I hated. Do anyone's hands get fully dry with a hand dryer? I didn't want to sit there like a dope for five minutes trying to get them dry so I ran my hands through my hair.

Looking at my reflection in the mirror, I stared deep into my eyes and gave myself a pep talk like I do before job interviews: "You can do it. You're going to fucking take this place. I believe in you!"

The blackjack table had two empty seats among a mixture of players. I was sitting at what I later called the international blackjack table. I was in between a guy from Holland and a guy from China, and there were two Russians across from us. It was like WWII, but the enemy (the dealer) was from Monaco. After playing for twenty or so minutes, our table started going on a run. We all kept winning. Every time the dealer dealt to himself I chanted, "Bust, bust, bust."

The Chinese guy caught wind of it and started doing the same but using the Chinese word "blast" instead of bust. All of us were pretty conservative with our money except the guy from Holland. He wasn't messing around, and had about three thousand Euro in front of him. After every few hands he nudged me saying, "If you want to win, you have to bet more than twenty Euro each time."

I looked down at my chips. "That's okay," I said. "I'm doing pretty well with the system I have."

I probably should have listened to him because we were robbing this place blind. I practically doubled my money in no time.

Soon, I was up to six-hundred Euro, but our run at the table had slowed to a jog and we started tripping all over ourselves. It wasn't just the bad cards. We had two unpleasant visitors arrive at our table. They weren't pit bosses coming to accuse us of counting cards, but something far worse: tourists.

An American woman in her late forties with a rock on her finger the size of a baseball stood at the empty seats with her "valley girl" daughter. I normally wouldn't care if people watched me play cards, but these yuppers were loud and obnoxious. I could tell by their over-excited attitude about being in a casino, that they had had a few too many Shirazes. After a few blown hands, the Russians bailed and walked away from the table. I figured that would be a good idea for me too, but couldn't help imagining my student loans paid off in Euros. "Do you want to play, honey?" the woman said to her daughter.

"Sure," she replied.

The mother took out a few hundred Euro from her Prada pocketbook and threw them on the table in front of the dealer.

"Chips, please," she said, as if ringing a bell for service.

The dealer rolled his eyes and exchanged the bills into chips. We resumed playing and our table continued its downward spiral. I lost eighty more Euro. God knows how much my friend from Holland was losing. The Chinese guy bailed next. The Chinese are good with numbers. He knew the statistics, and didn't let his dreams of buying a toy factory in China get in his way.

The American tourists weren't just awful at the simple game of blackjack; they were awfully annoying as well. Every time the dealer would win a hand the mother started making "boo" sounds. The worst was when the daughter got a nineteen or a twenty hand. She would say, "Take that, dealer!" I lost another few hands and decided to get out before all my winnings dried up. The guy from Holland followed suit, leaving the valley girl and her mother alone with the dealer, who was soon to make his quota for the month.

I was still substantially up, but decided not go to another table. I walked up to the cashier with a smile and dropped my chips on the counter. I changed it into hundreds, then went to the bathroom to put the money in my sock.

When I left for the bus I saw that it wasn't just my lucky day at the table. The bus pulled up right in front of the casino. Hopefully the train would be the same way.

Dirty Politics

When I got off the bus I looked up at the schedule for the Rome train. It was boarding in about a fifteen minutes and the next one was three hours later. My luck had continued. I guess I could have written down the schedules beforehand, but that's not how I rolled.

I walked up to the platform and sat down on a bench across from two girls my age wearing huge backpacks. One was skinny with light blonde hair; the other was much bigger with dirty blonde hair. The first blonde had a nice body, but her face looked like she'd been hit with a shovel. The dirty blonde traded her weight for looks, because she had a cute face. So basically they were both fuckable, but nothing to bring back to mom. The chubby one glanced over at me. "Are you American?" she asked in an American accent.

"I am. I suppose you are too," I replied.

"We are. What's an American boy doing in this luxurious part of the world by himself?" she asked.

"Gambling!" I said. "What are two American girls doing in Monte Carlo without pearl necklaces?" I said with a smirk.

"We're backpacking and came here for the day; not much here if you don't have a lot of money," the shovel-faced blonde said.

"I suppose not. Are you waiting for the Rome train?" I asked.

"Yeah, we're heading off to Rome. It should get in around 8:00 am," the chubby girl said.

"I took a night train to Rome a few weeks ago, and I think that's when my train got in, too."

"Was it nice?" shovel-face asked.

"The train ride? No, it fucking sucked."

"No, stupid," the shovel-faced blonde said. "Rome."

I thought for a second. "Well, the Vatican is amazing, but the rest of the city...well, it's wicked dirty."

I had only been in Rome for two days and breezed through the sites. Something about Rome had turned me off. Maybe it was all the stray cats or the black graffiti of swastikas sprayed on every other wall.

"So, it's nasty?" the chubby girl said.

"Yes, but I wasn't there long, so don't let that discourage you. I'm sure you'll have a good time."

She put out her hand. "My name is Kim, and this is my friend Alex."

I shook both their hands. "People call me Pile."

"What does Pile mean? Pile of shit?" chubby Kim asked.

"Pile of love baby," I said, trying to crack a joke.

The girls both laughed.

"Where in the States are you from?" I asked.

"We're from Michigan State. But I grew up in Ohio," shovel-faced Alex said. "Where are you from?"

"I'm from Boston. Where are you originally from, Kim?" I asked.

"Flint, so I pay in-state tuition unlike my friend here," she replied, pointing to Alex.

"Is Flint really as bad as the Michael Moore documentary?" I asked.

"There are a lot of poor sections there. My uncle used to work for GM when it closed down," chubby Kim said.

"Yeah, but he has a job now, right? It's not like he went crazy and started eating rabbits!" Alex chimed in.

I laughed because that part of the documentary gave me the creeps. "I'm not a big Michael Moore fan. Are you?" Alex asked.

"Not really. I think he's a rock thrower," I said.

"Oh my God, you're a Republican? You and Alex should date. No wonder you're in Monte Carlo," she said.

"I'm not a Republican. I'm pretty independent. Basically, I hate both parties."

"Who did you vote for in the last election? Don't tell me you voted for Bush?" she said.

"I did," Alex blurted in.

Kim rolled her eyes. "I don't understand, how can you support that warmonger, Alex?"

"The only warmonger was Saddam Hussein, who ran a fascist regime over his people."

The train then pulled up, so thankfully, I didn't have to watch the amateur Fox News debate anymore. I wondered how these two maintained a friendship despite such opposite political views. What was their common interest?

The girls put their huge backpacks on and we got on the train. They were struggling with them, and I could have helped, but I figured if they were backpacking they better get used to the heaviness. Plus chubby Kim could use the exercise. I followed them into one of the train compartments. "Do you mind if I join you?" I asked, even though I was already in the compartment.

"I insist," Alex said, winking.

I got that warm, fuzzy feeling that Alex was interested in me. I helped them put their bags on an overhead rack, then sat down underneath. I rolled my eyes up to look at the bags, hoping that they wouldn't fall on me. Maybe it was the dim lighting, but sitting across from them now, they didn't look that bad. "So, um, Pile, you're not really here gambling. Are you studying abroad?" Alex asked.

"No, I have an internship with these Italian artists. I'm helping them put together some art event."

"Impressive," Kim said.

"Nah, it's more like a vacation. But you can bet I'm putting it on my resume."

A woman in uniform walked into the room and looked at our tickets. They don't rip the tickets, just check them at every major stop. When taking a night train, it's something that gets real annoying. You struggle to fall asleep and the minute you do, there's someone in your face asking to check your ticket.

The woman looked at our tickets. "Merci," she said and left.

Kim smiled. "She was hot," she said.

"I agree," I said.

These two girls could be lezbos. "Are you two, umm...? Partners?" I said.

"No, we're straight," Alex laughed. "Well, I am anyway. Kim has been known to swing both ways."

"I'm bi," Kim said with a sense of pride.

"She's been hitting on me for years," Alex said.

Threesome?

This was starting to get interesting. When meeting girls, it's always good to find a way to bring sex and relationships into the conversation. That way, you don't waste any time and know where you stand from the beginning.

We went back into political talk. It was something I kept trying to avoid, because politics tend to divide people.

The political conversation finally hit a lull, mainly because I was playing devil's advocate with both of them. I decided to push the sex talk again. "So have you hooked up with any hot guys while traveling?" I asked.

"Not yet. Well Kim, you stole that boy away from me in Spain."

"I only kissed him. Why do you keep bringing that up?"

"I'm sure it would have gone further if you wanted it to," Alex said.

"Whatever. The kid lived with his parents and it's not like I could have brought him back to the youth hostel," Kim said.

Alex sighed. "So no guys yet. We brought a big box of condoms over because we thought we were going to do some fucking. But we haven't had a chance to even open the box."

My jaw dropped. Then a light bulb went off, and a triangle bell rang repeatedly like a wife calling her lumberjack in for supper. I had found a common interest between them that surpassed their divide politics: these two were slampigs.

"It's the condom curse." I said, laughing.

"What's that?" Alex asked.

"When you have a condom, you never get laid. Those opportunities always arise when you don't have one."

They both laughed. "So should I throw the box out the window?" Alex said.

They both smiled and looked at me like they were waiting for a witty response to come out of my mouth. I knew I had to do it. I had nothing to lose. I stood up and leaned into Alex's shovel face. "Fortunately for me, I don't have a condom. So as we say in Boston, let's reverse the curse."

I began to kiss Alex and she kissed back with no hesitation or embarrassment at having Kim right there. The kiss went on for a few seconds and I pulled away. We both laughed. Then I don't know what came over me. Maybe it was because I was independent and didn't want to choose sides. I looked over at Kim who was smiling, then leaned in and started kissing her. I knew she would kiss back; she seemed pretty slutty.

While kissing her, I got as excited as a puppy about to get a treat. When the kiss stopped, I went back to kissing Alex. Then I moved up to Kim and sat on my knees so I was a little under face level with her and started rubbing the sides of her breasts. I usually would start rubbing the side of a girl's stomach but I didn't want her to freak out at me rubbing her fat rolls. That is one thing I always took into account when hooking up with any girl who should hit the treadmill. Even though it's hard to resist, I'm very gentle, never rubbing any part of them that has blubber. It would make them feel insecure, freak out, and end your hook-up. I went back to kissing Alex and started rubbing the side of her breast as well.

After that, I felt like I hit a wall. I wasn't sure what I should do next. The questions rolled through my head. Should I keep this up? How long would this last? Should I go back to talking about politics?

Threesome?

Then I realized what I had to do if I wanted this sexual encounter to move forward. I took my hands and put them on the back of each other's heads and pushed them towards each other, hoping they would kiss. Kim leaned into Alex and started kissing her. It worked. I couldn't believe it – I was about to have a threesome. This was something every guy dreams about. The only difference was that these girls were gross. I watched the chubby make out with the fugly for about thirty seconds, then got back in on the action. I leaned between them and started kissing them both at the same time. We started to take turns but the whole thing was in sporadic seconds. It was so hot. Might as well go all the way.

I put my hand under Kim's shirt, slowly moving my way over her big belly, and fiddled around with her bra until it was unhooked. I started rubbing her breasts and she liked it. I moved on to Alex, putting my hands under the back of her shirt to disassemble her bra. Kim took her bra off from under her shirt and watched me finagle Alex's bra off. Once the bra was off, I put both hands up their shirts and we all started the three-way kiss again. I was in heaven. A boob in each hand and I didn't even have to pay any money for it. Suddenly, we heard the door slide open. We all stopped kissing and our heads snapped towards the door. "Bon...jour," one of the train workers said.

He had a passenger peering over his shoulder who was most likely waiting for the train worker to find him an open room. His eyes popped open at the sight of me on my knees with my arms under each girl's shirt. "Hello," I said almost forgetting my hands were glued on the girls' breasts. He smiled at me. "Pardon," he said turning around. He started to slide the door closed and I heard him say, "Américains fous," which is French for crazy Americans.

The three of us laughed at what just happened. I got on my feet and sat back in the chair. "That was fun. Thank you."

"Who said it was over?" Kim said.

She got up and sat down beside me and continued kissing me. I wasn't going to fight it, so I put my right hand back up her shirt and touched her breast. I grabbed her hand with my free hand and put it over my penis. Kim rubbed it on the outside of my pants then unhooked my belt and unbuttoned the button. The zipper opened up as she put her right hand in my boxers, taking out my erect penis. She started stroking it slowly. Yeesss, I said to myself. I opened my eyes and saw Alex with her legs and arms crossed. She looked pissed. "Shit Kim, you always do this too me!" she yelled.

Kim stopped kissing me and turned over to Alex. "What?" Kim said.

Alex got up and grabbed her huge backpack off the rack almost hitting me in the face with it. "Slut! That's what you are! A slut!" she yelled at Kim.

Alex slid the compartment door open and stormed out. Kim took her hand off my penis and got up. She grabbed a hold of the strap on her backpack and ripped it down off the rack. The backpack came down and hit the left side of my face. My head flew sideways towards the window. "Wait," Kim said.

Kim ran out the door after Alex, leaving it open. I paused for a second as my face started to hurt. I was sitting alone in a room on the train with my penis out. I put it away before anyone walked by and called the conductor. I couldn't fathom what just happened; my threesome vanished before my eyes. Looking back at the conversation regarding the boy from Spain, I figured the girls fought for guys like they did over politics. Who really lost though, was me, the independent.

7

Slampig

I had just returned to the States unemployed and homeless so I was forced to move into my father's house. To top off my lousy living situation, I had a huge student loan from Sallie Mae. Every other day that bitch was calling me up, trying to get the money I owed her for an over-priced degree in broadcasting. To overcome these problems, I spent my nights getting wasted at the local bar scene.

The Mug

At 1:40 A.M. when the respectable bars turn their ugly lights on everyone knows the only place to go for last call is "The Mug". "

The Mug is a little dive bar everyone drunk drives to, risking their lives for an extra twenty minutes of boozing. People don't just go for the strong rum and cokes that cost a dollar less than other places; they go for one last chance to hook up. The Mug makes sex happen for girls who don't normally have a chance. The slampigs get treated like queens, and it's always fun for us guys to lead a chubber into bed. But when you hook up with the girls of The Mug, it's best to go back to their house with a getaway car. That way, you avoid waking up next to some fat, sweaty Medusa living in her dysfunctional lifestyle.

That summer, The Mug must have had some financial problems because they waited until the final two minutes of the evening to announce last call. After everyone doubled up on drinks, the lights would come on and the bouncers threw everyone out. Even though I was in my twenties, I was the size of a sixteen-year-old and a noticeable mess when drinking. Because I stood out, I was caught by the tubby bouncer, Chris, and his cock-sucking sidekick Jimmy sneaking a beer out in my back pocket.

Chris was supposedly a madman in the 80's, but by now his muscle had mostly turned into fat from excessive drinking in the 90's, kind of like what was happening to my friends at the time. Jimmy was just an asshole. He was one of those bouncers who took the door job to his head and acted like he was guarding the White House. The next Friday when my buddies and I showed up, Chris stopped me at the door. "Not you," he said and stood in front of the entrance.

My loyal friends, Brownie and Lenny, laughed at me. "We'll see you in a little bit," Brownie said, leaving me outside to rot.

I was bullshit because I hadn't driven there and from what I could see through the window, The Mug was happening. Even though it killed me to do it, I had to make amends with Chris. If I was banned from "The Mug," I would miss out on many late night hook-ups. When Chris let the next group in, I walked up to the door to make peace. "Dude, Chris, I'm wicked sorry about everything. I just want to go in and hang out with my buddies."

"You pissed a lot of people off last weekend, Pile!" he said, pointing at my chest.

"How did I piss a lot of people off? You and Jimmy were the only ones that saw me."

"You told Jimmy to go fuck himself," he said.

I had been smashed and didn't remember saying it, but the guy probably deserved it. "Dude, I was really drunk. I won't even drink tonight. I promise."

Chris paused for a second. "Okay, I'm letting you in, but it's just because I know your cousin. Consider yourself on probation," he said and poked my chest with his finger.

Probation. Where did he think he worked, Studio 54? I wanted to flip his ass off right there, but I couldn't. The ball was in his court. And in his court there were slampigs to fuck. "Okay, thanks," I said and shook the fat fuck's hand.

I went in the bar and walked up to Brownie and Lenny. "How did you get in?" Lenny asked.

"I gave Chris a gift certificate to Dunkin Donuts," I smirked.

The group laughed and a few seconds later I was volunteered to get the next round of beers. Because things were cheap there, I didn't really mind. Until I opened my wallet and saw only a few crumpled bills. "Damn, I spent a lot of money tonight," I said out loud.

My plan in the beginning of the night was to stick to a budget by only drinking draft beers. All binge drinkers know that never ends up happening. Sure, you start out with a few two-dollar drafts, but as soon as the testosterone kicks in, you're giving the bartender your credit card for a round of Jäger shots.

I ordered three Budweisers and the bartender, Eddie, gave me a dirty look. "Are you behaving yourself?" he asked.

"You betcha," I slurred back.

He put three Budweisers on the bar. "Nine dollars," he said.

I handed him a crumpled twenty, which he took to make change. Eddie came back from the register and put the eleven dollars on the bar. "You know, if it were up to me, your ass would be banned for life. You're lucky Jimmy is in New Hampshire tonight."

I smirked. "I'll keep that in mind," I said, taking back my eleven dollars back, not leaving him a tip.

I gave Lenny and Brownie their Budweisers and took a sip of mine. They had just joined a group of our friends. After a few minutes of drunk talk, I had to piss, so I made my way to the bathroom. There was no line, but someone was in the men's room. After three minutes of wondering if someone had locked it shut, the door swung open. Two dirt balls came out sniffing. "Sorry about that kid. We had to take care of some business," one of them said.

I wanted to say, "Yeah right, scumbag!"

But after that night of almost getting my face beat in by a druggie with a "disability," I figured it was best to keep my mouth shut.

Inside the bathroom, I unzipped my pants and started pissing. What a relief. Then I thought of what cock suckers the boys of The Mug were and got angry. "The nerve of those motherfuckers," I said aloud.

I decided to be an asshole and started pissing on the floor. I laughed while spraying the tile. "I hope you enjoy cleaning up my piss, you fat fucks," I said.

I saw a small trash can on the floor filled with white paper towels and no plastic bag lining. I began to piss all over it, and in a few seconds the paper towels were clumping into wet yellow balls. I figured Chris and Eddie would have to spray the piss out with a hose. I nodded my head with pride. Suddenly, I felt a wetness in my right pant leg and shoe. I had stopped paying attention and pissed all over myself. I couldn't believe it. My jeans were soaked. Fucking karma.

I put my dick back in my pants and left the crime scene. I walked over to my friends and sure enough, Lenny spotted my wet leg. "Pile, did you piss yourself?"

Everyone laughed and so did I. "Yup, I had a little trouble controlling my wee, wee. It's huge, like a fire hose."

"You're fucked, kid," Lenny said.

Slampig

Brownie ordered another round. It was getting to be that time to either find a skank or go home to your hand. A Sox highlight reel came on the big screen TV and I looked over to see if we beat the Yankees. Then, at a table under the TV, I saw my future hookup. She was in her mid 30's, chubby, and pig-faced. Her hair was permed. It looked like her style was in transition between the Metal and Grunge era. She was sitting at an empty table sucking down some kind of mixed drink. I nudged Brownie. "I think I found who I'm fucking tonight."

"Yeah, who's that?" he asked.

I pointed over to her table. His face looked like he had just smelled a fart. "Dude, she's fucking gross," he said.

Slampig

I couldn't believe it: this from the guy who once fucked a girl who looked like the mother from "What's Eating Gilbert Grape." Whatever, I really wanted to hook up. I could tell she was a given, by the way her chubby face looked around the room for any signs of life she could take home. It would be like fishing in a fish hatchery.

I walked over to her table, pretending I was waiting for the final score on the highlight reel. When the score revealed the Yankees had smoked us, I clinched my fist. "Fucking Steinbrenner!" I said.

She looked up at me. "Right?" she said with a smile.

I knew she was going to be real easy. "Whatever, he fucking buys those rings every year. Someday his luck will end!"

She laughed. "Do you mind if I sit down?" I said, wondering why I was acting like a gentleman in an old black-and-white film.

The slampig looked up to me. "Only if you buy me a drink," she said with a Kool-Aid grin. I was shocked. The nerve of this hog, asking me for a free drink! I was a hot twenty-two-year-old kid. She was a gross thirty-something skank. But just like I had apologized to the bouncer, I came to my senses and realized the ball was in her court. And in her court, she was one of the few unclaimed pussies in The Mug. So I bit the bullet. "You're in luck," I said. "I'm on my way back to get another Budweiser. What do you want?"

She put her finger up to her mouth and thought for a second. "How about, um…how about a fuzzy navel."

"A fuzzy what?" I asked.

"A fuzzy navel. They're fab."

I figured it was one of those sweet, expensive drinks that would make me look gay just for ordering it. But if I could get a BJ out of the deal, it would be worth the label.

Saying the words "fuzzy navel" to Eddie the bartender made me feel like an asshole. But I got the Budweiser too, so I hoped it didn't look that bad. Because I hadn't tipped him the last time, Eddie went to the other end of the bar to make the drink. That meant there wouldn't be any booze in it. At first I was upset, but I realized this pig didn't need booze to get busy. Eddie came back with this girly orange thing and charged me nine-something for both. I paid, shook my head, and brought them back to the empty table. "Here you go," I said.

She sucked down the rest of her drink with the straw and grabbed the fuzzy navel like a kid would if you dangled candy in front of his face.

"Thanks, honey," she said, and winked.

Yeah, she could thank me by sucking my balls in Brownie's mother's Chrysler I wanted to say. "Are you old enough to be in this bar?" she continued.

I always got that. I looked like I was sixteen years old and numerous times I had had to provide a bartender with two forms of ID. "I actually turn twenty-three soon," I said.

"You could've fooled me," she said.

"So, I haven't seen you here before. Where are you from?" I asked.

"I grew up in Lowell, but have been living in Louisiana for the past year."

"What made you come back?" I asked.

"Cuz the father of my daughter is an asshole. So I'm staying with my friend in Lawrence until I get my shit together."

Right then, I should have gotten up and walked away, but my cock was doing the talking so I nodded my head and continued to put on my mack. "How old's your daughter?" I asked.

She went on and on about her kid while I was nodding my head and smiling. When she finally stopped, I continued my game. I looked her in the eyes seductively. "Your eyes are beautiful. They're like cocoa," I said.

I couldn't believe what was coming out of my mouth. Cocoa? I guess it was better than saying shit brown. After that, she looked at me like I was the captain of the football team asking her, the fat loser, to prom. Her foot started nudging up against mine and I went in for the kiss. Sure, if my friends saw it, I would be humiliated. But fuck it. I already had my leg drenched in my own piss.

We started kissing. She tasted like a mixture of an ash tray and an orange freeze pop. Then she stuck her tongue down my throat. It wasn't the soft French kiss that most girls kiss like; it felt like she learned her how to kiss in a women's penitentiary.

The "ugly lights" came on and Chris the bouncer started telling everyone to get out. Of course it was right after I bought two drinks.

I backed away from her slobbery mouth and took a good look. She looked like Sloth from the Goonies. I didn't care. I was going to try and get this girl to blow me in the parking lot. "Can I walk you to your car?" I asked.

"My friend drove, but we can meet her outside."

It took her three seconds to suck her drink down with the straw. I left my Budweiser for dead and we got up to leave.

We were some of the first people to go, which was good. It gave me a chance to slip outside with her before my friends saw us. I passed Chris the bouncer and said, "Goodnight."

Chris grabbed my arm and the slampig continued to walk. "Pile, every time I see you, you're trying to get with the grossest chick in the bar. You got no shame in your game, kid."

I looked over at her. She was so drunk she hadn't even noticed that I left her side. He was right. I was pretty bad. Regardless, I was still going to get head from this broad. "I don't know what you're talking about Chris. This bitch is dope," I said with a smile.

"Yeah right. Miss New England," he replied.

"Actually, I think she is from Kentucky," I said, laughing as I walked away. Chris was not one to be talking; he worked at The Mug. I was sure that he had invited far worse girls than Miss Kentucky back to his house for an after-party.

I caught up to my slammy and apologized for stopping. "Don't worry about it," she said.

We passed a big truck parked next to a cell phone store. I grabbed her hand and took her in between the building and the truck. She was all about it. The second we got out of sight we started kissing. Then she reached her hand down my baggy pants and started jerking me off. She stroked my penis in turbo gear. I wanted a blowjob, but beggars can't be choosers. A guy and girl walked by the truck and she stopped the jerk. "That's my friend," she said.

I was a little pissed now that I was going to have blue balls. This always happened with public hook-ups. I fixed my pants and we walked out toward an old, rusty station wagon. There was a couple outside waiting for her. The guy had a leather jacket, and I presumed from the emblem on the back, he was in a biker gang. He looked like someone I didn't want to fuck with. He had his arm around a short brunette. She was decent looking for her age. The only exception was her clothes. They were trashy as hell. They looked like she picked them up in a hurry from the clearance section at Wal-Mart.

"There you are, Tina," the brunette said.

She put her hand on my back. "This is my new friend. Oh, I'm sorry I didn't get your name," she said.

"That's right, we never exchanged names," I replied.

I shook the biker's hand first. If you're trying to hook up with a girl and there's a guy in her group, it's always best to be as nice as possible to him. Especially if the guy is a big biker. "What's going on man? My name's Pile," I said to him.

He shook my hand with one of those death grip handshakes that hurts. There's no need to shake someone's hand that tight, even if you're a big biker. "Aaron," was all he said in a rough voice.

With a name that feminine, no wonder he needed the strong handshake. The girl with the trashy clothes introduced herself as Donna. "Are you coming back to my house to party?" she asked me.

I looked at Tina. "Is that okay?"

"Why not?" she said and we all hopped into the station wagon.

In the backseat, Tina and I were smushed – not just because she was fat, but also because there was a car seat on one side. As Donna drove out of the parking lot, Tina started rubbing my leg, which was still damp from the piss. "Did you spill beer on yourself?" she asked.

"Um, yeah," I said with a smirk.

I looked over at the car seat. "This just ain't right," my conscience said to me.

Slampig

As we passed The Mug, I knew I made an awful decision by getting in the station wagon.

Aaron-the-Biker didn't waste any time in the front seat. He was all over Donna as she drove. He was rubbing her leg and tickling her, which twice nearly caused her to drive off the road. In the backseat, my slampig Tina continued rubbing my penis. The whole scene was making me sick to my stomach. After a few minutes of dangerous driving we pulled into a housing project. I knew it was a housing project, because when we were teenagers, we used to buy dime bags from a guy we called "Jamaican Joe," who lived in one of the units.

Donna pulled up next to a pimped-out SUV and we got out of the station wagon. On the way into the house, Aaron-the-Biker told me that he left his motorcycle at The Mug. "Are you crazy?" I said.

"It'll be fine. No one will fuck with it," he said.

Apparently, Aaron hadn't heard the latest car theft statistics in the city. A few years back, it was one of the highest in the country. I figured because he was in a biker gang he thought his bike was untouchable. Donna unlocked the front door and we followed her inside. I could hear the television on. I figured she had left it on so people would think she was home. That way, no one would break in for crack money. We all followed her into the living room and there was a skinny young girl with dirty blond hair on the couch in her pajamas. She couldn't have been older than eight years old. When Tina saw her, she stomped her leg. "Samantha! What are you still doing up?"

The little girl's eyes turned to fear. "Cameron was crying and I couldn't sleep."

Donna turned around and ran upstairs, past the biker and me. "You shouldn't be up at this hour. March your butt upstairs and get to bed!" Tina yelled.

"Yes, Mom."

The little girl jumped up from the couch and on her way out Tina gave her a hard smack on the bum, which made the girl run. Tina looked at Aaron and me. "My kid thinks she can do what she pleases."

There was an awkward silence, and Aaron-the-Biker and I looked at each other with a questionable look.

Donna came back downstairs. "Can you believe this shit?" Tina said. "It's 2:30 in the morning and my kid's up watching TV. Is Cameron alright?"

"She's in her crib sleeping," Donna said.

"My daughter, the little liar, just wanted to watch TV."

I looked back at Aaron again and he gave me another look. I think we both were thinking the same thing. These bitches were trash. They left a little girl to watch a baby and brought two guys back from The Mug. I think the scene made Aaron worried because he blurted, "Y'all got condoms?"

The two girls looked at each other and both said no. "Well, we need to go get some," he demanded.

I laughed in my head because usually the topic of condoms was a private thing. I think Aaron wanted to be sure that he wouldn't be the next "baby daddy." Donna took her keys out of her purse. "Come with me to 7-Eleven?" she asked Aaron.

Donna looked at me. "Do you have any money?" she asked.

God, what was up with these broads? I pulled out a five-dollar bill and gave it to her. She grabbed it greedily and took off with Aaron following.

The door slammed shut. Tina practically jumped on me. We were kissing and soon ended up on the floor. I lost my sex drive and lay down on my back. I was drunk, but tired-drunk, so I was ready to crash. I didn't even care if these two made it back with the rubbers. Tina must have thought that I stopped kissing her to talk with her instead, because she wouldn't shut up. On and on, she talked about her life. I didn't give a fuck, so I closed my eyes, hoping to open them again to the morning. Then I felt her paws undoing my belt. I opened my eyes and got grossed out at the sight of her trying to get at my goods. Though I had wanted a blowjob before, I'd changed my mind after seeing how she lived. She probably had sores all over her mouth. Great, now I'd get genital herpes as well.

She unzipped my pants and slid her filthy mouth down my soft shaft. Up and down she went and I wasn't getting hard. Getting hard was usually never a problem for me; the wind could blow and my dick would pop out like a jack-in-the-box. But not this time.

A few minutes passed and I still wasn't hard. I thought Tina would give up but she was a committed little skank. A minute or two later my dick started showing signs of life and perked up. Once it did, she mowed down like a hog eating its morning feed. A few seconds into her feeding, I started to enjoy it. My dick was throbbing in her mouth and I was about to bust a nut. Now came the part where we would see what kind of girl she was. A spitter or a swallower. I had my own prediction. But right before I could prove my hypothesis correct, we heard the front door open with drunken laughter. I patted her head for her to get off me. She slowly did. She may not have given a fuck if Donna and Aaron-the-Biker saw her eating cock, but I did. I pulled up my pants and sat up. Donna walked into the living room. "Here you go. You kids have fun," she said, throwing a condom on the floor.

She began to walk away and I got pissed. I gave this lady five bucks and all she gave me was one fucking rubber. "Wait a minute," I said.

She stopped and looked at me. "I'm gonna need more than one," I said.

"Yeah, right," she replied, as if I were a little boy saying he would grow up to be a professional football player.

"No, I am. Give me another one."

Donna pulled another condom out of the box of Trojans, tossing it to the floor. "Good luck, kid," she said and walked away.

I wasn't going to fuck Tina twice, but I wasn't about to be ripped off. I figured I should probably use the extra condom to double up. Who knew where this bitch had been?

I looked over at my slampig Tina and she was grinning. Most likely, she thought I was a fucking machine for taking a second condom. Tina got up, grabbed a faded pink blanket from the couch and laid it on the floor. On it were many stains that hadn't come out in the wash.

"So I guess this is it," I said.

This was probably, and hopefully, going to be the most grotesque beast that I would ever stick my penis in. We got on the blanket and started kissing. I took her shirt off. Underneath was a stretch-marked beer gut. I saw she was wearing a cheap tan bra that Donna had probably picked up for her at Wal-Mart. I un-hooked it and her saggy breasts flopped out, just like that fifty-year-old clean freak's had. On one was a faded rose tattoo. She stopped kissing me and stood to take off her pants and underwear. She was ready. Her beaver had a little stubble but her lips were sloppy. They looked almost like tentacles. Tina didn't have a full FUPA (fat, upper-pussy area) yet, but was starting to form a small fat pocket. Another year of eating mac-and-cheese on the couch would do the trick. She undid my pants, grabbed one of the condoms off the floor, and put it on my penis.

Tina lay down and waited to be serviced. I leaned over, adjusted the condom and put my penis in her. It went in with no resistance. The thing didn't even slide in; it just went in. I started to pump and found myself slamming air. She was moaning, but I couldn't imagine she was getting off with a pussy this loose. "Fuck me, come on, harder, yeah, harder," she said.

I was going to have to fuck her hard to feel anything from her hallway like vagina I was slamming. We continued for the next few minutes and I was surprised that I was still hard. It must have been her moaning which kept me erect. Tina grabbed the back of my neck. "Now fuck me doggy style," she said.

Ah, more work, I said to myself. I took my penis out of her sloppy goods and she flipped over onto her hands and knees. I saw a big, sweaty ass stain on the pink blanket and wondered if trashy sex explained the other stains, too. With her ass in the air, I could see how lumpy it was and groaned. I spread out the two lumpy cheeks and stopped before insertion. What I saw made me puke a little in my mouth. Her ass was poorly wiped and had what looked like an epicenter of shit surrounding her asshole. "What the fuck are you waiting for?" she yelled.

I swallowed the little bit of puke, put my penis in her, and tried to block her shitty ass out of my head.

"Oh yeah, I love doggy," she said.

I hoped this bitch is spayed, I said to myself.

After a few hard pumps, I slowed down and we started going through the motions like a married couple. I just wanted to blow my load and be done with this shitty mutt. I shook my head back and forth in shame. I stopped when I saw our reflection in the sliding glass door: her chubby, banged-up body on all fours with my young, skinny body slamming her from behind. It was a terrible sight. There was nothing romantic, hot, or even funny about it. I gave myself a dirty look in the reflected glass. I hated myself. My conscience started scolding me. "You're so much better than this," it said. "What are you doing with this lumpy, most likely, diseased cow?"

My conscience was interrupted by Tina's screaming. "Oh my God, I'm cumming!" she yelled.

I could feel her lower body shake, which made me forget about my guilt.

The vibrating slowed down, and I presumed Tina was finished. "I want you to cum on my tits," she said.

It was better than her vagina. I took my penis out of her and she turned around and sat up right. I took the condom off and started to jerk, aiming for the rose tattoo. About thirty seconds later I sprayed my semen all over her breast. Cum started to drizzle down the rose tattoo. Bullseye. After my penis was emptied of its suicidal soldiers, she lifted her left tit and took a big lick of the dripping cum. She put the saggy breast down and started rubbing the cum onto her tits as if it were sun tan lotion. My mouth dropped. It was one of the worst things I had ever seen. I lay down. "I need a moment," I said.

I looked up at the ceiling. What had I just done? The pig lay down and put her arm around me. "That was wonderful," she said.

I was so ashamed that I wanted to go home and cry. But I was stuck there. I was miles away from my house in a bad neighborhood. I couldn't even walk home. I looked over at the clock and saw that it was almost 4:00 A.M. It was impossible to call one of my buddies for a ride home.

Slampig

They were probably sleeping or too drunk to drive. Tina started to talk about stuff that I still didn't care about. On and on she went, about stupid shit like "goals" and "dreams." I interrupted her life plan. "Hey, I have to get home. Tell your friend to give me a ride," I said.

"We'll bring you home in the morning."

The morning wouldn't do. I had to get out of that housing project. "No, bring me home now!" I demanded.

"Just cuddle with me. We'll give you a ride anywhere you want to go in the morning."

At this point I knew there was no way out of there. So it was time to be a dick.

I stood up, put on my clothes and thought about when she asked me if I was old enough to be in the bar. Then I thought about my improv classes. "If I don't get home soon, my mother is going to kill me," I said, acting scared.

"What?" she asked.

"I'm only fifteen. I'm going to be in so much trouble," I said with puppy dog eyes.

"Shut up," she said with insecure laughter.

"I'm telling the truth. I'm a going to be a junior in high school this fall."

She looked me up and down. Because I did look like a junior in high school, her face grew terrified. "Are you really fifteen? Shut up, why were you at a bar then?"

"I took my older brother's ID. Miss, I'm sorry, you're going to have to get me home. My parents are very strict. They have to be, my dad is the chief of police in my town," I said, throwing another gem on the joke.

She got up and started pacing back and forth. "Oh my God, oh my God. What have I done?" she kept repeating herself.

I continued my improvisational scene. "You had sexual relations with a minor. That's what you did. Don't worry, miss. I won't tell anyone," I said with a Dennis the Menace smirk.

She stopped and I saw a tear trickle down the left side of her face. Although my improv instructor would have been proud, I knew I had crossed the line. I had pushed the joke too far. The tear turned to tears, and she started crying. Tina sat down on a wooden chair in the corner of the room, put her hands over her face and sobbed for a few moments. "Just kidding," I said like it was April Fool's Day.

She lifted her head and looked at me. "What?" she said, annoyed.

I walked over to the couch and lay down. "Calm down," I said. "I was just fucking around. I'm twenty-two. Goodnight."

I closed my eyes and fell sleep.

Morning

I awoke to a massive headache and Barney on the television singing some kind of number game. I sat up and saw that Tina's daughter Samantha was next to me on the couch with the dirty pink blanket wrapped around her. "Um, hello," I said.

"Hello. I saw you last night. I'm Samantha," she said. "What's your name?"

"Um, I'm Pile."

"You and my mommy had a sleepover. She usually sleeps in the same room with me. But I guess she slept downstairs with you."

"You guys share a room?" I asked.

121

"Yeah. Her, me, and my baby sister Ellen. Oh, and Cameron sleeps in Auntie Donna's room," she said.

"How many kids live in this house?" I accidently said.

Samantha paused. "Just the three of us. In my old house it was just me Ellen, Mommy, and Daddy. I had my own room there."

"Where was that?" I asked.

"It was in Louisiana. Mommy said we had to move because my daddy was bad. But I love my Daddy. I miss him."

"Where is he now?"

"He's still in..."

Tina came into the room and Samantha didn't finish the sentence. "It's time for breakfast. Come on, your cereal is going to get soggy."

Samantha jumped off the couch and ran into the kitchen. I felt bad for her. She didn't deserve to live like this. I looked at Tina. God, she was awful looking. This moment was exactly why I wanted to flee the scene last night. Tina looked at me for a few seconds. "Do you want some cereal?" she asked with an attitude, probably not over my practical joke yet.

"No, I'm just going to sit here and watch Barney," I said.

"Fine," Tina said and went back into the kitchen.

After a few minutes of watching Barney, I realized it was one of the gayest children's shows ever. Aaron-the-Biker walked into the room, sat down next to me and lit up a cigarette. "The fuck is this shit?" he said, pointing at Barney.

"I don't know. Some show Tina's kid was watching."

Aaron-the-Biker picked up the remote and turned to a hunting show on ESPN. "Dude, I need to get the fuck out of here," I said, hoping he would come to my rescue.

"I hear you, guy. Dona's almost ready to go."

"Is Donna your girlfriend?" I asked.

He laughed. "Fucking hell no! I just met her last night at The Mug."

We both started to laugh. "Looks like we made some shitty decisions," Aaron said, taking a drag off his cigarette.

"You don't even know," I said, referring to Tina's shitty ass. "Good call with the condoms."

"I'll say. I ain't paying for anotha kid," he replied.

Donna walked in the room wearing a faded Hard Rock Cafe Daytona Beach T-shirt. "You two ready to go?" she said.

Aaron and I jumped up as if our mothers had asked if we wanted to go to Friendly's for an ice cream sundae. We followed Donna out of the room and passed Tina in the kitchen scarfing down cereal. There were two babies, and Samantha sitting around Tina. Donna stopped. "Watch Cameron. I'm giving these two a ride back." Then she walked out of the house.

"Later," Aaron said to Tina with a smirk and continued following Donna outside.

Tina put her cereal bowl down, got up and walked towards me. Here it was, the big goodbye. I did the first thing that came to my head. I put my hand up. "High five!" I said.

She gave me a dirty look and a half-ass high-five. I walked out of the housing project and got in Donna's station wagon. The ride home was mostly silent. I was dropped off first. I couldn't complain but I really wanted to see if Aaron's bike was still at The Mug.

Slampig

When I got to my house I took one of those long, depressed teenager showers to try and wash off the invisible film that seemed to form over my body. In the shower, I vowed to myself that I would "never" hook up with another fat, trashy, undesirable chick again.

Grimace

I never was a big fan of New Year's. Most are spent at parties thrown by the only guy in town with an apartment. He always thinks he's going to have a rager but when no one shows up, his friends usually call it the worst New Year's party ever. And there is nothing more remembered than a bad New Year's party.

At these bad New Year's parties there are usually around twelve guys and two girls. One of the girls is hot, but her boyfriend is a big guy nicknamed Moose. The other girl is of course her chubby sidekick. Every hot chick has one. The personal self-confidence booster. It's just wrong. The hot girl is complaining about the number of assholes texting her and the sidekick is complaining about her asshole giving her swampass.

At these bad New Year's parties, the host always puts on CBS ten minutes before the ball drop. While everyone in Times Square is cheering with smiles on their faces, I analyze my New Year's and say to myself, "Hey, look they're having a good time. I'm sitting here at a sausage-fest about to drink five-dollar champagne out of a dixie cup." Then, thirty seconds before the ball drops, all the single guys start to surround the chubby sidekick, in hopes of getting some un-earned tongue.

By 2:00 A.M., Moose and his chick take off, leaving the chubby to have the time of her life in the closet with the best looking guy at the party. This leaves the rest of us who didn't get laid in a circle jerk playing the Cracker. The only funny part of the night is when the last guy to cum has to eat that salty biscuit.

There was one New Year's where I did get laid. Actually, I had a threesome. I did have to go to Montreal to do it, but unfortunately, the story wasn't like the ones in Penthouse Forum.

What Should We Do?

Party plans looked bleak for New Year's Eve. The only guy in town with an apartment had gone away with his family, so that was a bust. Plus, most of our friends were still in college and spent the winter break in their college towns. This left us "home town heroes" out of the loop. If we were smart, we would have gotten on the horn with one of our friends still in college and spent the night at UMass-Amherst or Plymouth State making out with drunken sorority chicks. But none of us were any good at planning.

That day I was at Scotty's playing Playstation with Andy and Rick. The continuing question came up, "What do you want to do tonight? We got to do something. It's New Year's Eve."

Our options were awful. We could go into Boston and hit up the clubs or watch the Three Stooges marathon. None of us wanted to pay a $100 cover charge for the Boston clubs. So it looked like we were going to ring in the

New Year with Larry, Moe, and Curly, until Rick got a called a girl from our town named Margaret.

A few weeks prior, Rick had slept with Margaret. You would have thought he took her virginity the way she wouldn't leave him alone. Over the phone, she told Rick she was heading to Montreal with her girlfriends who had a hotel room there. All we heard out of his mouth was "girls" and before you knew it we were bombing up I-89 in Scotty's Ford Explorer, drinking beer out of iced coffee cups.

For most of the ride Scotty had the needle pinned. The only time it wasn't was when another car blocked his way by going a measly 80 mph in the fast lane. That was when Scotty would ride their ass trying to get them to move over to the middle lane. If they didn't, he would flash his headlights and lay on the horn. Although Montreal was normally six hours away, we got there in a record four hours. Thank God for the beer in the iced coffee cups. If I wasn't buzzed, I would have ripped the "oh shit handles" off Scotty's Ford.

When we arrived in Montreal, Rick called Margaret. We met her and her friends at a nearby restaurant. All of them except Margaret were being real cunty. Luckily they were poor college girls, willing to share their room with us if we threw in some cash. Regardless of what Margaret's stuck-up friends thought of us, you could see that she was thrilled her prince charming would be ringing in the New Year with her. Little did she know that as soon as we got a spare key to the hotel room we would pull the ditch move.

After the ditch, we changed our money to Canadian dollars and walked into the first club we saw. It was called Club Boom and was filled with hot chicks - a real meat market. Before we went cattle rustling, we lined up the

Jäger shots to gain our confidence. After throwing them back, a fat girl walked by and cheered. Rick patted me on the back. "There's one for you, Pile," he said.

It was no secret to my friends that I had been known to throw it in fat chicks. But after banging that slampig Tina in the housing project, I had vowed to myself that I would stop lowering my standards. "Yeah right," I said to the group. "I told you before. I am going to stop hooking up with gross chicks."

"So it's kind of your New Year's resolution," Andy said.

"Pretty much."

"That's an impossible resolution," Scotty said.

The group laughed. "We should split up. Easier to get chicks in pairs," Andy said.

"Good idea," Scotty replied.

"Let's get another shot," Rick said. "Whose turn for buying?"

Scotty looked over at me. "Pile, don't you skimp out on us. You didn't pay for anything on the way up."

I bought the next round of shots and got suckered into a round of beers as well. Then we paired up. Andy took off one way with Rick. Scotty and I went the other way.

A half hour later, we all met back and none of us had had a bite. Scotty and I had a nibble, having a conversation with two hotties, but we split when their boyfriends came back with the girls' mixed drinks.

The place was still filled with hot chicks, but everyone was only interested in their own crews. So we did what most guys do when there aren't any girls to hook up with: we just got wasted. Scotty bought us a round of Irish car bombs. Those got me hammered and fired up. For the next twenty minutes, I went on a rampage trying to butt into groups and hit on chicks. My buddies were more embarrassed for me than supportive. One girl I talked to was black and had dreads. She vanished after I introduced her to Rick as Roberta Marley.

Happy New Year!

It was almost midnight and my drunk ass didn't see a New Year's kiss coming my way. Then my eyes zoned in on a fat slammy on the dance floor. She was dancing by herself and looked like an easy score. This wasn't just your average fat girl, though. She was tall, had short hair, a tight shirt and was HUGE. The size of a school bus. But I was drunk on beer, Jäger, and whiskey. Plus, the club's blacklights drew a lot of her slothy features away. I told my friends that I would be back and stumbled her way. Knowing my past, they knew exactly who I was gunning for. I could hear their heckling in the background but disregarded it, moving out to the dance floor for an easy make out.

I started dancing behind her and she happily danced back. After a few minutes she turned around and started dry humping me. I thought I should be the one dry humping her, but she was three times the size of me. Suddenly, the music stopped and an announcer came on over the intercom, starting the count down in French. It was ten seconds to the New Year and I was about to get an easy makeout with the fatty. I got myself amped up to go for it, then experienced a quick flashback of me doggy-styling fat Tina in the housing project. The night's earlier conversation came back to me. I could hear myself saying, "I'm going to stop hooking up with gross chicks."

I came to my senses and decided to go another New Year's without kissing a chick. I had just started to walk

away, when the announcer said, "Trois, deux, un! Bonne et
heureuse année!"

Confetti showered down from the ceiling. The fat
girl grabbed my shirt and planted a sloppy kiss on me. I
instantly kissed back. Fuck it.

We started making out. Scotty was right; it was an
impossible resolution, especially because it was broken the
first second of the New Year. As she slobbered all over me
in the middle of the dance floor, I figured I should just
make the best of the situation. I stopped kissing her and
grabbed the fat rolls on her back. "Let's go somewhere
quieter," I said.

The fat girl led me upstairs to the top part of the
club where there were far fewer people. We found a
discreet place behind a railing to lean on and started going
at it. She sucked my lips, then inhaled my tongue. I was
worried that her instinct to eat would take over and claim
my tongue. I wanted her to calm down, but she then started
rubbing my cock and got me excited. I sucked on her neck,
then released before a hickey set in. "I want to fuck you,"
the gross pig whispered to me.

I stopped. Even though she was the size of a
rhinoceros, I was still down for a quickie. "Do you have a
hotel room close by?" I asked her.

She stopped for a second and looked into my eyes.
"Fuck me right here."

I looked around, wondering how I was going to
accomplish this. Sure, there was no one around. But she
also had jeans on. How do you fuck a girl in jeans? If she
had a dress, I could pull her drawers down and fuck her
from behind, but I wasn't going to strip her down and go at
it. If someone saw her with her pants down, we would get
thrown out. Worse, it would be an eyesore to the public.

I pulled out one of the three condoms stuffed in my wallet. I wasn't sure if she counted as reversing the condom curse. I unzipped my pants and put one on under my boxers. She bent back on the railing and I pulled the front part of her pants down a few inches. I tried to stick my dick in her, but it didn't work; the condom got fucked up. I adjusted the condom and tried again. "If this is going to work, I'm going to have to lie down," she said.

"What, are you crazy?" I said. "We'll get thrown out of here."

"No one will see, just fuck me."

"I'll keep trying this way," I said.

She rolled her eyes and leaned back again.

After about five unsuccessful attempts I took off my condom and threw it on the ground. "Will you give me head?" I asked.

"No, I don't do that right away," she said.

I wondered why she would fuck me in a club, but not blow me. Then I realized that she knew our sexual encounter would end after I came. I'm sure a fatty like her has had enough experiences giving guys head and watching them ride off into the sunset. You can't blame her. She wanted some satisfaction as well. I was going to have to do it her way. It would be ballsy, but kind of like grabbing a case of beer out of a delivery truck: in and out in seconds, the whole thing over before anyone noticed. I put another condom on and told her to lie down. She pulled her pants down and lay on her back. I got on top of her massive body, inserted my cock under her FUPA and started thrusting as fast as I could. This was so fucking retarded.

I fucked her hard so I could get off before some French-Canadian security guard threw me into the streets. The only way I was going to cum, though, was to block these thoughts and just go for it. She started quietly moaning in my right ear, giving me that phone sex satisfaction that would make me cum. Right before I did, I pulled out, got up on my knees and jerked myself off a few strokes to let the semen fill up the condom. Then we heard a bunch of people cheer behind us. "Oh fuck," I said.

We turned around to see a group of college kids. This frat boy pointed at me. "One-minute man!" he yelled, referring to the Missy Elliot song.

Someone took a picture with a disposable yellow camera and I freaked. I quickly ripped off my condom, threw it on the floor, zipped up my pants, and started pacing away. The frat boys tried to hi-five me, but I hung my head in shame. A pretty girl standing with them looked at me in disgust. She couldn't believe what she had just seen. "You got to love Montreal," is all I could think of to say.

The group gave one last cheer as we walked past.

I could feel myself start to sweat. I was about to have a panic attack. We walked by the men's room. "I have to go to the bathroom," I said.

"I'll wait outside," the fat girl replied.

"I would rather you just fucking go away," I wanted to say.

I went into the bathroom, headed directly into a stall, sat on the toilet, and ran my hands through my sweaty hair. I couldn't believe what had just happened. "Calm down kid, its okay, its okay, get a grip," I said to myself.

After a minute or two of almost hyperventilating, I had a reality check. I had just fucked a behemoth in a club without getting caught. The whole thing was funny. Calmer now, I walked out of the bathroom hoping the fat girl was gone so I could go rally the troops. Within seconds, she jumped in front of me like a DWI roadblock. "I can't believe we just did that," I said to her.

She gave me a flirtatious look. "I can," she said. "That was hot. I'm still sweating."

You're sweating because you're a fat pig! I wanted to say.

Of course I was sweating too, but I was pretty sure it was a cold sweat. I looked at her circumference and felt ashamed again. I hadn't learned anything since Trashy Tina and her shitty ass. We got a beer and for the next few minutes it was hard to talk about anything. If she was hot, maybe I would have been all lovey-dovey. But she was gross. I knew I had to ditch this pig. If I were at her house I could look at my watch and pull the usual "Listen I have a big day tomorrow." But here I was at Club Boom in friggin' Montreal. I was stuck.

After every question she asked, I responded with a quick yes or no answer. I knew she could tell I wanted to make a break, and that was good. She must have been through this before, because she kept her pride and said, "I need to go find my friends."

"Yeah me too," I replied.

This girl was giving me a break. Now all I had to do was find my friends and get the fuck out of there.

"Maybe we can meet back later," she said with a questioning look.

"Maybe," I echoed. But the way it sounded, I might as well have said "probably not."

"Maybe your friends and my friends can all hang out later."

"Sure," I said, hoping the two groups would never cross paths.

She was most likely with other girls, but hell, my friends were shit out of luck. If we had been with her friends before, sure, I would have fucked the girl just so my buddies would have a chance. But I had jumped on the grenade before she'd even been tossed into my group's bunker.

We split up in different directions. I circled the whole club, but couldn't find my group anywhere. That feeling of anxiety I'd had in the bathroom came back. My friends had left. I didn't have a room key, and worst of all, I didn't even remember where Margaret's hotel was. My cell phone service had dropped as soon as I crossed the Canadian border. Scotty's cell phone worked in Canada but where was there a pay phone? I wondered if he would even answer. I decided that I would walk around one last time before I figured out how to call Scotty's phone.

Scotty

I paced back towards the bathroom and there was Scotty, walking around too. I was so relieved I almost cried. For a split second I felt like a lost child in a supermarket who had just found his mother. Scotty didn't quite feel the same. He pushed me and I flew back a few feet. "Where the fuck have you been? I've been looking for you for a half hour."

Still thrilled at being rescued, I took a few heavy breaths. "Dude, I just fucked that fat chick."

"Shut up!" he said.

"No Scotty, I fucking did."

"Where?"

"Here. I fucked her in the club!"

Scotty lifted his head. "Get the fuck out of here," he said.

"Dude, it was up in the top area of the club. She was fucking nasty."

"I don't believe you."

Right as he said that the fat girl came up behind me and tapped me on the shoulder. I turned around and almost jumped in fright.

She was joined by two of her friends, a guy and a girl who seemed like a couple. Scotty looked the fatty up and down. "Pile's told me so much about you," he said.

You had to hand it to Scotty; he didn't give a fuck about anything.

The fat girl smiled at him. "What has this boy told you?"

"Pile told me that you two share common ground."

The fat girl started laughing and put her hand on my shoulder. "We shared a common ground alright," she said, winking at Scotty.

Scotty's eyes lit up like the Fourth of July and he started laughing. She introduced us to her friends and we chatted a little. They seemed hesitant to talk and I could tell something was up.

The fat girl's girlfriend gave her an ultimatum. "We're going back to the hotel. Are you coming?"

The fat chick looked at Scotty and me. "What are you two doing?" she asked.

I stumbled over my words, trying to think of an excuse. But Scotty chimed in first. "We're going to meet our friends at a strip club. Do you want to come?"

I had no idea why he just invited this sloth out. All I could think was that he wanted to show the guys what I'd been doing for the past half hour.

"I'll go to a strip club. That sounds like fun," she said.

She turned to her friends and whispered something to them. I presumed it was about her taking off with us. I said in Scotty's ear, "You are a fucking asshole. You know that?"

He laughed and we all walked outside. The street was lit up with real lights, so unlike the club's everybody-looks-hotter blacklights. Naturally, the fat girl looked grosser than ever but I noticed something else besides her ugliness. It wasn't the blacklight inside that had made her hair look purple. Her hair *was* purple. Scotty saw it and nudged me. "Pile, your girlfriend's got purple hair," he said.

I smirked. "Yeah, she looks like that purple McDonald's character. What was that things name?"

"Grimace. You fucked fucking Grimace," he said, laughing.

While the guy in their group performed boyfriend duties by hailing a cab, Grimace and the other girl argued – probably about Grimace going with us. I hoped she would go back to her hotel. When the cab pulled up, the couple got in and left, not even saying goodbye. They were pissed, but I didn't care to ask Grimace what the fight was over. Looking back now, I should have inquired, using it as an angle to get her to leave.

As soon as the cab pulled away, Scotty took charge. We walked by a number of strip clubs on St. Catherine's Street. Trashy Canadian guys were outside waving flyers and yelling things like, "The girls will ride you like you're a horse."

"What club did the guys go to?" I asked Scotty.

"The Tiger Cage," he replied. "But I don't want to go there. I want to go to the one my cousin told me about."

We walked a few more blocks and came to a place called the Enchanted Forest. The club looked beat and I was sure the strippers' forests weren't going to be very enchanting. Scotty led the way into the club like he was Ray Liotta in Goodfellas. He shook the bouncers hand and we followed him into the main room. The place was the size of my dad's basement and the girls on stage looked like crack-whores. The doorman said something to us in French, then Scotty tipped him. He thanked Scotty and arranged a table for us up near the stage.

Grimace sat in between Scotty and me with an impressed look on her face. The doorman asked if he could get us all a drink. Scotty asked for a round of Budweisers, then looked over to Grimace. "Is Bud okay?"

I wondered why he even gave a fuck.

"A Budweiser would be great," she replied.

"My type of girl!" Scotty said, slamming his hand on the table.

He then slapped his hands together. "How about these seats, Pile?"

"The girls look like they belong in a basement of a church talking about what they used to do for money," I said.

"Oh come on, Pile. They're not that bad."

Watching the show, I realized that strippers in Canada are a lot different than strippers in the States. They will do anything for a few Canadian dollar coins. Like Europe, Canada has dollar and two-dollar coins. There are no bills until you get to a five. And no one is going to give any one of those crack-whores a five unless they plan on sucking them off. So people threw coins at the stage and the strippers picked them up with their vagina lips. I wondered what would happen if one got lodged up there. It would make for an interesting talk at the gynecology office.

The doorman came back with three Budweiser pounders and Scotty tipped him again. He must have tipped him generously because the doorman had a big smile on his face. "If you need anything, just ask," he said.

He walked away and we started to watch the show. I took a sip of my pounder, looked to my right and suddenly there was a stripper in a chair beside me. She almost startled me because I hadn't seen her sit down. Our eyes connected. "Bonjor," she said in her French accent.

"Hello," I said back.

She smiled. "I like you. You go in the back with me for ten dollars?" she asked.

This is the part I hate about strip clubs. It's hard to say no to these cock-teases when they offer you a lap dance. But lap dances are the biggest waste of money. They sit on you, get you hard, then walk away. It's like watching a porno with your dad; a boner for nothing. "What do I get for ten?" I asked.

She ran her hands down her sides. "You can touch my body."

She squeezed her breasts. "You can touch my tits."

Then she stuck her finger in the air and wagged it. "You cannot touch my pussy," she said.

"Maybe we can go in the back room a little later," I replied.

She got up. "I'll be waiting," she said, walking away.

I watched the stripper walk away and saw she had the ass of an eighteen-year-old girl, which nearly changed my mind. Then there was a loud smash and she jumped back a few feet. I looked to my right and saw two drunken douchebags fighting. A guy in a Yankees hat swung at the other, who had frosted highlights. When the punch connected, the frosted highlight guy fell back into a waitress with a tray of mixed drinks. The waitress flew back towards the front of our table and tried to gain her balance to save the drinks. Just when I thought she had saved them, the tray slipped out of her hands and three glasses of what looked to be rum and coke dumped all over Grimace. The bouncer came over, grabbed both douchebags and escorted them out like they were misbehaving children. Two small groups followed the bouncer out and I wondered if there would be a fight outside.

I looked over and saw Grimace was soaked with booze. She looked down at her shirt and lap. "What the fuck?" she said.

The doorman ran over to our table with towels and he and the waitress started to wipe off Grimace. They apologized over and over. After they cleaned up what they could, the doorman leaned over to Scotty. "You all can have a lap dance on the house," he said.

We all started talking and a waitress came over with a round of pink shots. She lined them up on the table. "Compliments of the house," the waitress said.

Grimace picked her shot up. "This will make me feel better," she said.

She put it back without even flinching. Scotty laughed. "That's my girl!" he said.

I wondered why Scotty was being so friendly to Grimace. He must have just been eating up the situation. He loves spontaneity.

Scotty and I followed her lead and threw back our shots. It was sweet, but I still washed it down with Budweiser. "I think I'm ready for a lap dance," I said.

Scotty looked over at Grimace. "Are you ready for one?"

"Fuck yeah! Do you want to come with me, Scotty?"

"Sure," Scotty said, slapping his hands together for the second time that night.

We all got up and Scotty told the doorman that we were ready. He escorted us to these tiny rooms in the back that looked like cubicles. The doorman said something to a bouncer and then asked us which girls we wanted. "It doesn't matter," Scotty said.

I wanted the girl who talked to me earlier, but wasn't going to be picky because the whole thing was free. The doorman waved three girls over.

I walked towards one of the cubes with a skinny blonde in a gold slip dress. Scotty said something to the strippers and all four of them went into a cubicle room together. I wondered how they were all going to fit, especially because Grimace would take up half the room. It wasn't my problem, I thought, and sat down in an empty cube. The stripper started dancing around me. She didn't waste any time taking her slip off, then sat on my lap with her back facing me. She threw her hands back, grabbed mine and put them on her tits for me to rub. I was so excited to actually be touching someone other than Grimace's breasts that I rubbed them more like someone pets a puppy. When the stripper started rubbing her G-stringed ass up on me, my cock became instantly hard. A few moments later she flipped around to face me and started rubbing my rock-hard dick outside of my jeans with her vagina area.

She was dry humping me. This was far better than the dry humps I received in the dating scene, and far better than Grimace's on the dance floor. "Don't be afraid to grab my bum," she whispered in my ear in her thick French accent.

She steadily accelerated her dry humping and I would have probably cum if I wasn't so astonished at the quality of my lap dance. Back home, a lap dance was like you were Santa Claus and the girl was sitting on your lap asking for a new Barbie. But this girl's body continued to thrust on mine and even though she had a thong on, I could feel her pussy lips spread out over my cock. "You're making me so wet, fuck me, fuck me!" she kept saying in my ear.

I started to move my crotch area in sync with hers. A few minutes later we slowed down and she got off me. "You need to clean up?" she asked with a smile.

"Almost," I said reaching into my wallet to give her an American twenty.

It was kind of a big tip for a stripper but I had never had a stripper do anything like that before.

I left the cubicle area and saw that Scotty and Grimace were making out at the table. That dirty dog, I knew it.

I waited until they were finished and sat down beside them. "How was your dance?" Scotty asked me.

"Incredible," I replied. "You?"

"Awesome!"

I looked over at Grimace who was next to me. "And yours?" I asked.

She smiled. "It was a tease. You know I like to go all the way," she said with a wink.

This girl was a fucking pig! Since I just saw Scotty making out with her, I had a feeling she would be going all the way with him by the end of the night.

I lifted what was left of my Budweiser pounder and took a sip. As I did, Grimace started to kiss Scotty again. They stopped a few seconds later and Grimace looked over at me and giggled. I gave a small smile and Grimace leaned in and started kissing me. When she was done, Grimace quietly said in my ear, "Scotty is making me choose."

Scotty overheard this and laughed. "Choose! You think I care? We'll both fuck you."

Grimace smiled and paused for a second. "Hey, what happens in Canada stays in Canada, right?" she said.

"Right, let's go!" Scotty said, like she had just signed her soul over to the devil and it was too late to go back.

Wait, What Are We Doing?

On the way out the door my mind started racing. There was no real reason for me to fuck this fat girl again. I had already busted my nut, and got a supreme lap dance. Did I really need to double stuff this Macy's Day blimp with Scotty? Grimace staggered behind which gave me a chance to talk to Scotty. "Hey, I'm all set with banging this chick again. Where are we even going to do it?"

Grimace wondered the same thing, because right after I said that she asked, "Where are we going?"

"No questions!" Scotty said in a stern tone, but looked back at her and winked.

This was one of the many times where I questioned why I hung out with Scotty.

I stopped and let Grimace catch up while Scotty led on like General Patton driving his tanks through Europe. "Scotty, seriously, where are we going?" I said.

"Oh for fuck's sake, Pile. We're going to Margaret's hotel to get my car and drive to another hotel. Is that okay with you?"

"We should try and get a room at Marg..."

Scotty cut me off. "Negative, Margaret's hotel is booked. Andy already checked."

I looked over at Grimace. "You don't have to do this if you don't want to," I said, hoping she would change her mind.

"It'll be fun. Plus, you two are hot," she smiled.

Like most situations with Scotty, I was in this until the end.

We arrived at Margaret's hotel and were just about to ride the elevator down to the parking garage when we saw Rick and Andy with Margaret and her friends walking in the lobby towards us. I almost shit when Andy spotted us. I could care less about Rick and Andy seeing us with Grimace, but they were with Margaret. If Margaret saw us with the fatty, what happens in Montreal would not stay in Montreal. Scotty saw them too. "Oh shit," he said quietly.

The elevator door opened. "Hey, where are you going?" Andy yelled.

Before I knew it, Scotty pushed both of us into the elevator, jumped in and hit the button to close the door. I heard Andy let out a howling laugh as the door closed. "What was that all about?" Grimace asked.

"Um... I don't know?" Scotty said, giving me a funny look.

We got in Scotty's car. I sat in the passenger side and Grimace sat in the back, probably taking up a seat and a half. Scotty drove out of the garage and was all over the road, using his cell phone to call Canadian information. We got the numbers of five hotels. His cell phone bill must have been as enormous as Grimace, because not only did he call Canadian information, but he called all five hotels looking for a vacant room. Luckily, the last one had one available room left. He booked us into a Holiday Inn under his name.

Hotel

After a few minutes, we made it to the hotel. Scotty parked in a visitor's spot and we walked through a revolving door into the lobby. He told Grimace to have a seat while the two of us went to check in. "Scott Lavato here," he said to a French Canadian behind the desk.

The guy asked if we had a reservation and Scotty said yes. He typed something into the computer and asked Scotty to repeat his name. "Scott Lavato," he said, a little aggravated.

The hotel attendant typed the name again and nothing came up. "Shit, friend, we called a few minutes ago!" Scotty yelled.

"I'm sorry. We don't have any reservations under your name."

"Well, book us another room!" Scotty said, pissed off.

"I'm sorry, the hotel is full."

Scotty put both hands on the table. "This is bullshit we just called five minutes ago! Get me your manager!" he yelled.

The guy rolled his eyes and went into a back room. I tried to straighten Scotty out before he started breaking stuff. "Scotty, fuck this. Let's just go."

"No, Pile, we are going to bang this broad if it's the last thing we do."

I started to plead. "Just fucking do it in the truck. Go! I don't even want to fuck her. Take her back to the truck and bust a nut while I get something from the snack machine."

The hotel attendant came out with another person who I suspected was the manager. He looked like he was half asleep and asked for Scotty's last name. "Lavato, for fuck's sake. Scott fucking Lavato," he yelled.

The manager typed in the name. "Yes, Room 312. Let me get a key for you," he said.

He started talking in French to the other guy and showed him something on the computer. When he went to get the key, Scotty and I came to the conclusion that the hotel attendant must have been typing in "Scott" for the last name.

The manager came back with our hotel key and we flagged Grimace to get her fat ass up from the couch. We walked to the elevator and rode it to the third floor. When we arrived at 312, Scotty slipped in the key card and opened the door. "Finally. This is gonna be fun," Grimace said.

Scotty and I let out a few small chuckles. "What, you didn't have fun at the strip club?" Scotty asked.

"And what about me? You didn't have fun at Club Boom?"

"Well it's hard to have fun when it's only a minute long," Grimace said with a smile.

Scotty roared laughing. "You just got burned," he said.

We walked into the low-budget hotel room. There were two beds but no couch. This meant Scotty and I would have to draw straws to not cuddle with Grimace after the deed was done. Grimace went to the bathroom and Scotty and I sat on the two separate beds. "Don't puss out on me, Pile!"

Anyone who didn't grow up with Scotty would have questioned the psychology of the situation. Why was it such a big deal to have me fuck this girl at the same time as him? But Scotty wasn't gay, nor was he one of those sick fucks that like seeing their wives fucked by a stranger. No, Scotty was just an asshole and thought it would be funny to give a fat girl a double stuffing.

Grimace came out of the bathroom and looked at Scotty and me. "Are you guys ready?"

I kind of felt like we picked up a hooker up and she was on the clock. "You bet," Scotty said.

I looked down at the floor. "How about you?" Grimace said to me.

"I'm ready," I said as I looked up.

"Let's get it started, shall we?" Scotty said.

Grimace took off her shirt. Seeing her with her shirt off made me want to puke. She had big tits, but her gut stuck out as far as her breasts. She lunged onto Scotty's bed like Yokazuna, and I thought Scotty was going to bounce upward and get his head stuck in the ceiling like in the cartoons. They started kissing heavily. Then Grimace stopped for a second, grabbed me and pulled me onto their bed. She started kissing me and ripping off my shirt. This girl was a wild boar. Scotty laid her feet out, unbuttoned her pants, and yanked off her jeans. He then took her ginormous wind sail panties off. I stopped kissing her and looked at the big blubbery FUPA that I'd felt in the club. Her pussy was shaved which actually made it worse to look at. I normally hated hairy beavers, but looking at it big and bare grossed me out.

There was no shame in Scotty's game. Seconds after Grimace's panties were off, he pulled his pants and boxers down to his knees. He climbed over her enormous leg and started fucking her. I couldn't believe that he didn't put a condom on. He was raw dogging this girl and loving it. I sat there by her head, looking down at her Rocky Mountain body and watching Scotty slam her as I had at the club. This confirmed to me that when it comes to fucking a fat chick, all us guys are the same. We try to get off as quick as possible.

Grimace started moaning. "Yeah, fuck me. I want to cum!" she yelled.

Scotty suddenly stopped. He pointed his finger at me like he did to the hotel desk worker. "Pile, get in the game!" he yelled.

Grimace turned her head towards me. "Stick your cock in my mouth," she said.

This sounded like a good idea. That way I could get off and not have to fuck her again. I unzipped my pants and pulled my boxers down resting them under my testicles. I wasn't hard because watching one of my best friends bang a fat chick was nothing to get excited over. I hesitated for a few seconds. "Stick it in her mouth, Pee-Wee!" Scotty said.

I knelt beside her head and she started sucking my limp dick while Scotty continued fucking her.

It took a minute or two for my cock to get hard in her mouth. It probably would have been sooner if Scotty hadn't been talking dirty to her, saying things like, "Do you like the suck and fuck? You do, you naughty little girl, you."

Little girl was an understatement. My mood switched abruptly to fear when Grimace was about to reach orgasm. As Scotty humped the shit out of her, she moaned with her mouth gagged on my dick. Louder and louder at every pump, her mumbled moans continued. I needed to pull my cock out of her mouth before she came and bit my dick off.

Luckily, Scotty came before she reached her peak, saving my cock from being John Bobbitted. He let out a loud "uhh," and stopped fucking her. My eyes blew up when I saw that he hadn't pulled out and cum on her. He came in her. Scotty got up from the bed. "Finish her off," he said, looking at me.

He lay down on the other bed and reached for the light switch. "I'm going to sleep," he said, dimming the lamp by the bed.

The blowjob had stopped and my dick was just resting in her mouth. She most likely was thinking of what an asshole Scotty was, but I was sure this wasn't the first time a guy had done this to her. She spit my cock out of her mouth. "Well, you gonna fuck me or what?"

I really didn't want to, but I could tell by the tone in her voice, she was more than a little pissed at Scotty. So I figured it was time for me, Mr. Nice Guy, to show her a little affection. I put a condom on because I wasn't going to end up on Jerry Springer with Scotty. I began fucking her and gave her the shittiest sex anyone has ever given anyone. After a few dull minutes of barely getting any moans from Grimace, I basically fake-came. I pulled out, took the condom off and threw it on the floor. I wiped the condom slime off my hand with the blanket, hoping it was the lubrication and not Scotty's cum. We both got under the covers and Grimace looked over at me. "Damn, you suck in bed," she said.

I could hear a small laugh from Scotty's bed. I sighed and turned the other way. Before drifting off to sleep, I looked at the digital clock. It read 5:40 A.M.

A Few Hours Later

A few hours later I woke up to hear Grimace whimpering Scotty's name. "Scotty, Scotty, you need to wake up," she kept saying.

I figured she wanted either to go another round or to "talk" to Scotty to let him know she really wasn't a whore. Regardless, I was still drunk and half asleep, so I didn't give a fuck. I turned in the other direction and tried to go back to sleep. "Wake up Scotty," she said again.

This was starting to become an annoyance. She tapped me on the shoulder. "Kyle, Kyle, wake up!" she said.

I laughed to myself, because she thought my name was Kyle. Then she grabbed my arm and started shaking it. "Kyle."

"What?" I exclaimed, rolling back over.

"You need to wake Scotty up; I need to get back to my hotel. My friends are leaving in an hour," she pleaded with me.

I then felt certain sympathy for this girl. She probably thought we were just going to fuck her and bring her back to her hotel. She continued to try and wake Scotty up. "Scotty, Scotty, wake up," she whimpered.

I sat up. "Scotty!" I yelled.

Still nothing, so I repeated myself louder. "Scotty, wake up!"

Scotty quickly sat up and pointed at me. "I fucking heard her, Pile, that's the problem!" he yelled.

He was hung over and didn't want to deal with the repercussions of Grimace. Grimace practically got down on her knees, knowing he was her only hope. "Scotty, I don't want to be stuck up here. My friends will leave me."

"Some friends," Scotty said.

"Please, Scotty, please," Grimace said.

"Fine, let's go," he said, throwing off the covers.

He started to put on his pants. "Well just don't sit there, let's move!" he yelled.

We put on our clothes and followed Scotty out of the hotel room. Closing the door, I saw a practically spotless room, with two messy beds and a soiled condom on the floor.

In the lobby, we all walked towards the front desk, until Grimace made a beeline for the all-inclusive continental breakfast buffet. I saw there was a new guy working the desk. "Room 312, we're checking out," I said.

Slampig

Scotty clenched his fist and slammed it down on the counter. "Pile, why are we up right now? We should be sleeping!"

He started banging his fist over and over on the counter. "What did I do to deserve this?" he yelled.

I looked back and saw Grimace had stopped putting food on her plate to watch Scotty's outburst. He buried his head on the counter like an upset child who refuses to work in class. The hotel worker ignored Scotty and told me the room cost a hundred and twenty dollars. My mouth dropped. It seemed pretty foolish, all that money for a few hours. I took out my wallet and shuffled through the money. Scotty's head was still down on the counter. "Um, Scotty," I said, hoping he had money to split the bill. "Scotty," I repeated and his head shot up.

"Oh, for fuck's sake," he yelled.

He pulled out a pile of crumpled Canadian tens and twenties, threw them on the counter and walked outside. I unraveled the bills and found they were more than enough to pay his half. After I paid the bill, I walked over to the continental breakfast for an apple. Grimace was shoveling an everything-bagel with a thick spread of cream cheese into her mouth. A horn honked in the background. I looked outside. It was Scotty and the horn didn't stop. I looked over at Grimace. "We'd better go," I said.

The ride back to St. Catherine's Street was pretty quiet. The only talk was Grimace giving directions to her hotel. Scotty pulled up to the front of the hotel, almost hitting the curb. "Thank you. It's been fun...well kind of," Grimace said.

Scotty turned toward the back seat. "Be good," he said.

Grimace got out, and Scotty sped off.

We drove toward Margaret's hotel to pick up Rick and Andy. The silence continued. At a stoplight, Scotty looked over to me. "Did you like that little show I put on at the hotel?" he asked.

"Show? It was a show all right. A fucking shit show," I said.

The light turned green. "Oh Pile, you didn't think I was serious, did you?"

"Well you were being a bitch."

"I came in her."

"I saw."

"A fat girl like that will take any chance she gets to have a baby."

I felt bad, so I humored him. "Yeah, they train for it by being nannies and working in day care. How many fat girls have you met who work in day care? They do that because no one is stupid enough to fuck them without a condom…Well, except you," I said, laughing.

"This one time, you are absolutely right. Showing her what a madman I was, was my only card. Having her see that shit show, she would be crazy to keep my child. She'd think she was spawning the antichrist."

His alibi sounded good, but I didn't believe him. He was truly freaked out back at the hotel, but not to just to make Grimace believe he was a madman. He was freaked out because someday Grimace would be back on his doorstep with a fat baby.

The ride home sucked. Even with about six Red Bulls in him Scotty almost fell asleep at the wheel. Rick took over and his driving wasn't any better. I could have sacked out but couldn't stop thinking about my New Year. I thought about how I fucked Grimace in the club. I wondered if the surveillance people would see it on the security tape and post it on some porn website under the category "skinny guy fucks fat chick in club." I realized my life was terrible. My whole life I called girls slampigs, but I was the slampig. I slept with anything that moved. I really needed to stop being an asshole and find a girlfriend. I looked out the window so the guys wouldn't see my eyes water.

I was relieved when we pulled into our hometown and not into a casket. Within a week, the word spread about Grimace. But it wasn't Andy who told everyone. It wasn't even Rick and his offensive mouth. It was Scotty. He told everyone in town about our night. But he left out one minor detail. He left out the fact that he was involved and told everyone that I fucked a huge girl without a condom.

9

The Cheat

I moved to Albany, New York to work at a radio station for a few years. I loved my job but it literally paid the same as bussing tables in high school. In radio, unless you're Howard Stern or Don Imus, you barely make enough to get by. Sure, chicks are impressed when you tell them your job title, but what good is that when your piece of shit Honda is broken down off the side of the highway at 4:00 A.M.?

The few cents an hour above minimum wage forced me to get a second job at a trendy coffee shop. Working at this coffee shop was the gayest experience of my life. All the employees were homos, including the girls. Because I was young and boyish looking, they all thought I was gay too. That is, until my girlfriend Stacy came in one day for her caramel macchiato. After she kissed me on the lips, I heard a slight whimper from my co-worker Jeff. After that day, all the gay guys treated me differently because I wasn't gay. So basically, at this coffee shop, I was the minority.

Stacy was my second girlfriend. She was great until our relationship changed. Every day was an emotional dilemma and I was convinced it had to do with the night she hung out with "a friend". First of all, any time your girlfriend says "a friend," it refers to a guy. Second, any time your girlfriend says she "hung out" with "a friend," it means there is something more than friendship. Any normal person with nothing to hide would say "my friend Betty," or "my friend Ann," or even "my friend Mike." But if you cut it short and use "a friend," it could be a fuck friend.

By the end of the summer, I knew I needed to make a life change. I realized I would never break $20,000 a year working in radio. So I enrolled at a college back in Boston for my Bachelor's degree. As much as I wanted Stacy to care that I was leaving, she didn't. We simply decided to stay together until I left for college. I was fine with that because deep down, I still really liked her and hoped that love would emerge in the end.

The Last Days

I gave my two-week notice at the radio station for reference purposes, but at the coffee shop, I didn't give a fuck. They were getting a two-day notice, and in my opinion, they were lucky to get that. I was planning to take Stacy to Boston to show her where I'd be living and more importantly, have one last hurrah with her. So, I conveniently made my last day at the coffee shop a Thursday. My manager was new and overworked, so I knew she would be pissed. On Wednesday afternoon, I came in a little early to catch her before she went home. I went into the back room where she was stocking coffee cups. "You're in early," she said.

I didn't waste any time. "Yeah. Hey, today and tomorrow will be my last days of work."

Since those days were Wednesday and Thursday, she knew I was sticking her with the weekend shift. Her face turned red. "You're screwing me!" she yelled, pointing her finger in my face.

I didn't care about people yelling at me, but hated having a finger pointed in my face. I got nasty. "As much as we love our jobs here and act as if we're a family, we're not. In reality, this is just a glorified retail position and you, as a manager, should be prepared for the revolving door of retail employees," I said, wondering if I should close with "how do you like them apples."

She turned around and was silent. I had crossed the line and hoped she wasn't getting ready to throw something at me. "Start your shift. I'll deal with the paperwork tomorrow," she said quietly.

She would have fired me on the spot, except that would mean she'd have to cover my shifts. And when you're a manager, there is no overtime; you're on "salary."

The next night, I looked at my watch: in two hours my shift would be over and I'd hang up my apron for good. After what I said to my manager, I probably wouldn't be allowed to step foot in their store again. My soon to be ex-co-worker Cathy walked in, presumably looking for a free coffee. Cathy was a hot lesbian, who my girlfriend and I had hung out with once at a Tori Amos concert. I liked Tori Amos, but her concert was as gay as an AIDS rally. "Hey Cath," I said.

"I hear it's your last day."

I smiled. "Word gets around fast."

"Jeff called and told me," she said. "You know, gay guys love gossip."

I laughed because she was right. Gay guys are worse than old ladies.

"Well, Cath, I want to stay. I do, it's just that I think going back to college is the best decision."

She laughed. "You don't have to justify your quitting to me. I'm not your mom," she said.

I was going to miss Cathy. I was always under the impression that lesbians were bull dykes in crew cuts who hated men. But I was wrong. Lesbians were pretty cool, especially Cathy.

"Can I make you a drink?" I asked.

"No, its okay, you make a shitty cappuccino. I came in to see if you wanted to get sushi tonight."

I managed to suppress a joke about lesbians wanting to eat fish.

"That would be great. I just have to call my girlfriend and make sure it's okay."

Cathy paused for a second. "That's understandable," she said softly.

"I've never had sushi," I said.

"Then you're in for a treat. This is the best place in town."

I didn't take her word for it. The whole idea of eating raw fish kind of grossed me out but if it was a respectable Asian restaurant, I was sure they'd have some crab rangoon for me. Cathy took out her cell phone to look at the time. "I'm going to go run some errands. You get out at nine, right?" she asked.

"Yup."

"Okay, I'll be back around then."

Cathy left and I called Stacy. The phone rang a few times, then Stacy picked up. "Hey," she said.

"What are you doing?" I asked.

"Just chatting on Instant Messenger."

I was curious who she was chatting with. "Remember that lesbian I work with?"

"Which one?" Stacy asked, laughing.

"The one from the Tori Amos concert?"

"Yeah, she was probably the only lesbian at the show who didn't hit on me."

"She asked if I wanted to get sushi after work. Do you want to come?"

"No. That girl's crazy. I'm just going to stay here. I need to clean my apartment anyway. Call me when you're done and we'll talk about Boston. Okay?"

"Will do."

I hung up the phone and started to close out my shift.

Cathy came back ten minutes before my shift supervisor had to lock the doors. She knew Cathy and I were going out, so she let me off early even though it was against policy. The only reason I'd stayed as long as I had was that my shift super was cool and I didn't want to fuck her over. The thing about retail is that your allegiance is with your co-workers, not your company. I put my hand out to say goodbye. "Nice knowing you!"

"Good luck," she replied, then looked at Cathy. "When are you in next?" she asked.

"Tomorrow afternoon."

"Me too!" she replied. "See you then."

We walked out the doors. "I took the bus here," Cathy said. "We can take the 455 to the restaurant...unless you want to drive." She waited hesitantly for me to take the bait.

"Now, who's taking who out?" I said with a chuckle.

Sushi

We walked into a small, empty sushi bar. Any deserted restaurant that serves raw fish is a red flag. When we sat down at our table, I ordered a beer and Cathy ordered water. The Asian woman said, "Just water?" She gave an angry look when Cathy said, "Yes, just water."

That made me want to take my beer order back and get my own water, but I figured if they were serving us raw fish, we should be polite. I didn't need to get food poising before my trip to Boston.

I saw that there was no crab rangoon on the menu and got pissed. What kind of place was this?

I let Cathy order the meal because I didn't have the faintest idea what a California roll was. Somehow we started talking about anxiety and anti-depressants. "I don't know. Everyone gets upset. I don't think people should take drugs to fix their problems," I said, being very skeptical about the whole anxiety phenomenon.

"What do you mean?" Cathy said.

Then my asshole side came out. "I think people need to toughen up and stop acting like a bunch of pussies."

Cathy's jaw dropped. "How can you say that?"

"It's true. Our generation has become a bunch of babies and we use anxiety as an excuse for everything."

Cathy's attitude did a 180, from lovable lesbian to crazy bitch. "You have no idea what it's like to go day to day, not knowing if life is going to get better," she ranted.

I hoped she was joking but when I saw her eyes start to water, I realized this lesbian was nutty. "Hey, Cath, Cathy, I was just messing around. I'm sorry I didn't realize..."

She cut me off. "How could you kid around like that? You barely know me on the other side of the counter."

"Yeah," I said, rolling my eyes.

My attitude had flipped as well. I couldn't wait for the dinner to be over and go back to my girlfriend's house. Stacy would get a kick out of this story.

"So are you seeing anyone?" I said, hoping to get us out of awkward land.

"Not at this minute. Why? Do you know anyone who's interested?" she said, giving me a wink.

This girl must be bipolar as well as nuts, I thought.

"Um, not really. I was just wondering."

Cathy then let out a sigh. "I don't really care much for monogamous relationships. No offense."

"None taken," I said, taking a sip of my beer. "They can be tough sometimes, but they're worth it."

Cathy sighed again. "Not sure they're worth all the hassle."

The waitress arrived at our table with the sushi, which didn't look that bad. I just wasn't sure how someone was supposed to get full off those little circles. Cathy picked up her chopsticks, plucked up one of the pink-centered-rice-seaweed things, and put it in her mouth. "Mmmmmmmm," she mumbled while chewing.

Well, here goes nothing. I picked up something I thought was tuna. The sushi slid off my sticks. After a few failed tries, Cathy laughed. "Use a fork," she said, picking up another piece of sushi with her sticks like a pro.

"No, I'm getting the hang of it," I said.

I poked through a fish circle with one stick and used the other to scoop it up. The second my teeth bit through the seaweed and rice, I closed my eyes in disgust. I chewed it like a child being forced to eat broccoli. Then I thought of what I did when my mother forced me to eat my vegetables. I took a big swig of my drink and swallowed the food like a pill. The raw fish crept down my throat.

Cathy smiled. "It's good right?"

"Yeah, not that bad," I lied.

"Try the salmon," she said.

If there was one fish I hated, it was salmon. And the thought of having to eat it raw made me want to vomit. But I did my best. As I tried to force one down, Cathy made orgasmic sounds chewing hers. All I could think of was the fake orgasm dinner scene in "When Harry Met Sally."

The dinner didn't last long considering there wasn't much to eat at the table. When I found out that the shrimp and the California rolls were cooked I hogged them and left the raw fish for Cathy. I'd had enough of this night. I planned to drop this lesbian off, go to my girlfriend's house, and beg her for sex. Cathy and I both dropped twenties on the bill and I was relieved to be done with the night. "Let's go get a drink. Ever been to Charlie's?" she asked.

"No. I've never been there."

"It's great. You'll love it."

I didn't know how to bail without being rude. So I didn't. "Um, I just have to call my girlfriend," I said, folding under pressure. "Maybe we can pick her up..."

Cathy rolled her eyes. I was getting the feeling she didn't like my girlfriend.

I reached for my phone as we approached the car, but it wasn't in my pocket. I hoped it was in my car and not the restaurant. I opened the car door. "Hold on. I just need a minute outside," Cathy said.

"Are you alright?" I asked.

She put her hand on her stomach. "I'm okay. I just have a hard time digesting. Just give me a second."

I saw my phone on the car seat and picked it up. There were five text messages. Before I could open them,

Cathy started throwing up onto the curb. I rushed over to her side. "Just a minute," she said, then threw up again.

I wasn't surprised at what I was seeing. In the restaurant, Cathy had shoveled down that raw fish like an escapee from a WWII Japanese prison camp. I didn't want to make her uncomfortable so I took this opportunity to look at my text messages. All five were from Stacy. They went like this:

9:42 Hey, how's dinner?

9:52 Are you there?

9:58 Where are you?

10:03 I don't know about going to Boston tomorrow.

10:09 I'm going to bed!

I didn't care about the rest of the texts, but the one about not going to Boston pissed me off. She was so impulsive. We had plans and I knew she was going to break them. If she told me the day before, I wouldn't have burned my bridge at the coffee shop and made a few extra bucks before leaving.

While Cathy dry-heaved, I called Stacy. She picked up the phone on the second ring. "What's up?" I asked.

"How's your dinner?" she asked in a bitchy tone.

"It sucked. And this girl is puking in the street. I'm going to drop her off. Can I come over?"

There was a pause. "I don't know. I guess if you want. But I'm in bed. It's kind of pointless."

I was used to this act by now. Usually I pulled my gay "but I want to spend time with you" act. This time, though, I wasn't having it. I held my own. "What is this shit about you not wanting to go to Boston? We've been planning this."

There was another long pause. "Its not that I don't want to go, I just... I just have a lot going on," she said, waiting for my response.

I was fucking pissed. "A lot going on? You play on Instant Messenger all day talking to God-knows-who! And here I am, rolling out the red carpet for you. You know something, you can go fuc..."

She cut me off screaming. "I have a lot going on! My house is a mess. My life is a mess, and I don't want to talk to you right now!"

She hung up the phone. That was it. I had lost her; I tried so hard to keep the flame going. But it hadn't been enough.

I walked over to Cathy to see if she was done throwing up. "Are you alright?" I asked.

She was sitting on the curb. "I think so. Just a little embarrassed."

"Don't be. I've seen many girls throw up. Just not over raw fish."

"It's not the fish. I sometimes have trouble keeping things down. I heard you yelling. Is everything alright?"

"Relationship problems. It's nothing."

"That's why I don't have one," she said in an "I told you so" voice.

The street light cast a soft glow on her face. "Let's go get that drink," I said, hoping she could be a shoulder to cry on.

"You know, I have alcohol back at my house. Why don't we go back there?"

I thought for a second. "Why not?" I said, opening my Jeep door for her to get in.

The Lesbian's Den

Cathy lived in an apartment a few blocks away from a college, on the same street as some of the frat houses. School was starting that upcoming Monday and the streets were littered with kids drinking. There was a party in just about every duplex. We found a spot and I wondered if I was going to come back out to find my Jeep windows smashed. We walked past frat boys yelling with wobbly girls in their arms. Cathy's house was one of the few dark houses on the street. "Are your roommates in college?" I asked.

Cathy paused walking up the stairs. "No, my roommates are older."

I wondered if that meant her roommates were her parents.

That theory was cut short when I walked into a psychedelic house. Every door had a bead curtain and the ceiling was hung with numerous tapestries of suns and moons. I felt like I was in some kind of hippie commune. I looked toward the kitchen and saw a scruffy guy with greasy hair wearing a beat-up Grateful Dead shirt. The best part was that he was in his underwear drinking water from a Brita pitcher.

"Oh, hey," Cathy said.

The guy in his underwear quickly took his mouth off the Brita. "Cathy, I didn't hear you come in," he said.

He walked over to me, Brita still in hand, and put out his free hand for me to shake. "I'm Lester, one of Cathy's roommates. Welcome," he said, in a soft creepy voice.

Where had she found this meatball hero? "Les, this is the kid I was telling you about. You know, the kid I had a crush on," Cathy said.

I stopped for a second, then it all dawned on me. This whole night had been a set-up. I had just been on a date with a girl I thought was a lesbian. But I guess like most lesbians, she wasn't an official lesbian – meaning there were just some things a woman's tongue couldn't do. More importantly, this meant I was at her house not for a drink, but for a fuck. I came back to my normal state of mind and pretended that I hadn't heard what Cathy just said. I shook Lester's hand. He said, "Well, I have to go back to bed. Nice meeting you. Mi casa, su casa."

"Um, de nada," I replied.

The guy was a fruitcake and I thought he was gay until I found out that Cathy's other roommate was his wife. I didn't get to meet her, but I bet she was a real space cadet.

Lester walked up the stairs by the living room. Cathy opened up one of the kitchen cabinets and pulled out a five-dollar bottle of champagne, the kind you buy for the seven people who show up to your crappy New Year's party. She smiled at me. "I've been saving this for a special occasion."

She winked at me and I got a little bugged out. The night had started oddly and I wasn't sure how it would finish.

Although my relationship was obviously on its way out, I wasn't sure if that banging Crazy Cathy was the right move. Cathy popped the cork and quickly poured the champagne into two mugs. One said "Ft. Myers, Florida" and the other had playing cards on it. Cathy handed me the playing cards mug. "What should we toast to?" she asked, lifting her mug.

I gave a confused look. "Um, ah, what about..."

Cathy interrupted me. "I was thinking fate," she said pushing her mug towards mine.

I should have just walked away right then but I didn't.

We knocked our mugs together and a small amount of champagne spilled out of mine. We both took a sip. Cathy licked her lips. "Mmmm, I love champagne."

It tasted like piss. I'd have to shoot it back, because I would never finish taking little sips like this. The girl really knew how to pick food and drink.

"Let's go over to the couch," she said.

This was it. This was where I would choose my destiny.

I followed her to the couch and sat down. While she talked about some stupid shit, I weighed the pros and cons of fucking her. She was hot, but she was crazy. She'd thrown up just an hour before, but again, she was fucking hot. The fact remained. I would be cheating on my girlfriend. Of course, my girlfriend was a bitch who had probably been cheating on me throughout our whole relationship. So I went for it. I kissed her. Cathy softly kissed back. Her mouth tasted like the cheap champagne. After a few moments, she pulled away. "I thought you'd never kiss me," she whispered.

I rolled my eyes and kissed her again. In a few moments she started nibbling my lip. I put my hand on her stomach and worked my way under her shirt, lightly touching my way up to her breasts. Her body was nice. I unstrapped her bra and massaged the outside of her nipples. She gasped. "I've wanted you for so long. The way we connect at work, I want us to connect physically like that," she said.

This weirded me out but my penis didn't care. It was rock hard and about to break my pants zipper. Cathy ran one hand up my leg and over my erection. "I can see you've been waiting for this a long time too."

This girl was fucking nuts. There were definitely going to be repercussions. Thank God I'd soon be fleeing the state. Cathy unbuttoned my belt and unzipped my fly. Then she dug her hand into my boxers and pulled out my penis. I felt like I was going to cum right there. Cathy put her other hand on my chest, nudging me to lie down. I did and she put her mouth around my penis. I closed my eyes as she started licking the shaft and stroking it. "It tastes so good in my mouth," she said.

She sucked my penis a few more moments then sat up. "Let's go upstairs to my room."

We proceeded upstairs. All my worries about fucking a crazy girl evaporated. I just wanted to go upstairs and tear this girl apart. She shushed me as we walked past her roommate's door, then led me into her room. It was practically empty; the only thing in there was a futon and some clothes on the floor.

I sat on the futon as Cathy closed her door. She then lunged on me like a lion. We kissed heavily all over our bodies until she started biting my neck. I quickly grabbed her shoulders. "No biting," I said softly.

That was all I needed – to show up at my girlfriend's house looking like I'd been attacked by a vampire.

"But you taste so good. I want to bite you all over."

Biting was fun and all, but girls who bite in bed have something wrong with them. Once our shirts came off, I was grabbing her firm breasts and sucking her nipples. Cathy fell back on the bed. "Fuck me. Fuck me like you've wanted to fuck me all this time at work."

Apparently, I'd been sending her mixed messages, because all this time I'd thought she was a lezzy.

I took her pants off. She had no underwear on. Her box was hairy, but not Nancy the Neat-Freak hairy. I went down and started sucking, causing her to pant heavily. She grabbed my head. "Put it in me. Do it now!"

I pulled my jeans down to my knees and placed my cock in her vagina. It was so moist, my dick didn't feel the slightest resistance. I pumped a few times, enjoying her warmth, until I came to my senses. It killed me, but I had to put a condom on. I could easily see myself wanting the most out of Cathy's pussy and stupidly nutting in her. When I pulled out, Cathy snapped out of her enjoyment and looked at me. "What are you doing? Why did you stop?"

"I have to put a condom on."

"No, no, no condom! It feels so good. Just put it back in."

"Are you on the pill?" I asked.

There was a long pause. So even if she said she was, I wasn't going to chance it.

"I'm not. Just pull out."

"Easy for you to say," I said, rolling my eyes.

I took my jeans totally off and fished my wallet out of my pocket. Cathy gave me a bitch sigh. I took out a Durex condom left over from when Stacy and I had first started fucking. I put it on, inserted my dick into Cathy and started to fuck her hard in the missionary position. After I got tired, Cathy got up and rode me fast and steady. A few minutes later she closed her eyes and threw her head back. "Ahh fuck, I'm cumming!" she said.

The instant she said that, I came myself, harder than I ever had in my life. I grabbed her ass and pulled it into my crotch, so she could feel my penis pulsing. She stopped and soon got off me. I took off the condom and threw it in a small trash barrel. I lay down on my back and she curled up next to me. "That was great," she said.

She closed her eyes and in a few seconds fell asleep. Lying there next to Cathy, I felt proud of what I had just done and figured breaking up with my girlfriend would be much easier.

Morning

I woke up around 9:00 A.M. and started to quietly put on my clothes. I was planning to slip out the door but stubbed my toe on her futon, which woke Cathy up. She sat up and the sheet fell off her breasts. They were so nice I wanted to grab them and go another round, but figured it was best to leave in the morning without showing much emotion. If you have no feelings for someone, it's best to leave as a buddy, not a lover. "Are you leaving?" she asked.

"Yeah, I need to do some shit today," I said.

"Well don't forget about us at the coffee shop."

"I won't," I said.

I leaned over and kissed her goodbye on the cheek.

While walking out the front door, I could have given myself a high five for how perfect everything went. There wouldn't be any repercussions to fucking that crazy chick. I'd just had no-strings-attached sex with probably the hottest chick I would ever be with. And now I was ready to leave my bitchy girlfriend behind and go back to college. The whole world was ahead of me. The only time I'd look back would be to pull the image of Cathy's naked body out of my crank-bank to give myself a good whacking.

Around noon, I got a call from my girlfriend. She apologized, and I said I was fine with her not wanting to go to Boston. "I still want to spend our last days in Albany together happy," Stacey said.

At this point I didn't care. In my mind Stacy's behavior had led me to cheat, but figured if I ended our relationship the right way. I could always have someone to fuck in Albany.

The Last Night

My last night in Albany, Stacy and I decided to go out to eat and spend the night together. On my drive over to pick her up, I stopped to get an iced coffee. On my way out of Dunkin, I checked my phone and saw that I had a missed call from a number I didn't recognize. I played the voicemail, thinking it was probably a bill collector or something. Unfortunately, it was Cathy.

"Hi, this is Cathy. I hope your life is well. Listen, this is going to sound weird but I was hoping to get your girlfriend's number."

I dropped my iced coffee on the ground. "What the fuck?" I said aloud.

The message continued, "I know its weird, but you're a cool guy so I figured it's only natural that your girlfriend's cool, too. I didn't get to know her at Tori but would like to. So give me a call at this number or just text me hers. Okay, bye."

Was she fucking serious? I wasn't sure what to do. Who does that? Did she want the number to confess? Or did she really want to hang out with her? And even if she did, I was sure a loon like her would spill the beans.

Logic told me to ignore the call but I wanted to smooth everything over. Sure, Stacy and I were coming to an end, but it was still for the best that she never know that I cheated on her. .

I called Cathy and she answered in a few rings.

"Cathy. Why do you really want her number?" I said in a strong tone.

This probably wasn't the best approach because she snapped back at me. "I'm just looking for someone to hang out with!"

I didn't believe her. "I'm not giving it to you," I said nastily.

"Why not?"

"Um, jeez Cath, I don't know? Why don't you figure it out?"

"What? Because of us. I won't tell her," she said.

"Sure you won't," I said sarcastically.

There was a pause. "It doesn't matter, I'll see her."

I stopped for a second. "What does that mean?"

"It's a small city I'm bound to run into her. Plus, she comes in for her caramel macchiato all the time."

She hung up the phone and I knew I was doomed. I tried my best to bury that the fact that I had a crazy mistress, and to pretend everything was normal on my last night with my girlfriend.

Going out to eat with Stacy calmed me down. When the two encountered each other, Crazy Cathy probably wouldn't want to make herself look like a slut by telling the truth.

That night, I lay in Stacy's bed thinking. I came to the conclusion that I shouldn't have cheated, but I did what I did, and wouldn't ever do it again. In the morning Stacy's alarm blared the fact that it was time for her to get up for work and for me to go to Boston. She switched the alarm off and lay there with her head turned to the wall. Then I heard a small noise come out of her. She was whimpering. "Stacy?" I said.

She turned over to me and I saw she was in tears. "I don't want you to go," she cried. "I'm sorry for being mean to you. I just got scared. But now it's too late. You're leaving."

I had never experienced this before, that black-and-white film moment where someone cries over me, telling me how much I meant to them. But I didn't feel the way I wanted to feel. Stacy leaned over and hugged me. "I don't want you to leave," she said.

"I thought you didn't like me anymore," I said. "I actually thought you cheated on me."

"Cheat on you? That's ridiculous. I love you so much," she said. "I don't want this to end."

Stacy buried her head in my shoulder and I could feel her tears running off me. I closed my eyes and shed my own tears. But it was from guilt.

10

The First Friday II

Going back to college when you're older, you notice things you weren't aware of when you were younger. The first thing is that you realize you're sitting in class with a bunch of burnt out, zit-faced kids. The whole period, they stare at the clock, in hopes the professor will let them out early. These kids look pitifully at someone like me as "the old guy in the back." They're thinking, "Good for him for doing something with his miserable excuse for a life." Then they go back to watching the clock.

Another thing you notice is the actual worth of college. Lectures are a bit harder to sit through after you've spent time out in the real world earning every penny. You listen to some professor whose closest contact with the private sector was some internship he got in 1972, and the words "total bullshit" come to mind.

Regardless, I was having a good time. I was in my late twenties but looked somewhat young, so I didn't get that many stares on the first day of class. When the students got to know me and discovered the number of presidential

172

elections I'd voted in, they started to wonder if I was a NARC.

I moved into Rick's apartment, and didn't make a lot of money, which meant the federal government filled my pockets with financial aid. It seemed every time I looked in my mailbox there was another check I hadn't worked for. Sure, I would have to pay it back, but I'd worry about that later.

I decided to give the dating scene another go, but I passed on a lot of the college bimbos. Don't get me wrong, I still slept with your average slammy. But I felt it was time for me to grow up and find someone qualified. The problem was that trying to date career girls when you're a student in your late twenties is a tough sell.

Friday Night

It was a Friday evening and Rick and I sat around the apartment with no idea what to do. I picked up the "Improper Bostonian" (a city entertainment guide) off the coffee table. Flipping through the pages of a guide to find some Friday night entertainment was a real sad moment in my life. I realized I had grown up and wasn't cool anymore.

I found an ad for "The First Friday" at the museum and laughed. "This is tonight."

"What?" Rick said.

"We can go here," I joked as I showed him the ad.

"Isn't that where you met that old lady with the big bush?" he asked.

"Yeah."

"Dude, let's fucking go!"

I sat back for a second. What the hell, it would be a riot bringing Rick to this event. He was such an asshole.

Sticking him in a room full off oddballs would be a memorable experience.

We arrived at the museum late, so there was no line at the door. At the counter, Rick paid the full admission while I took out my college ID for a student discount. The attendant squinted his eyes at me, double-checking the college ID to make sure it wasn't expired. My face turned red. Yet another sad moment in my life.

We walked though the doors into the main hallway. The scene had not changed. It looked like a Halloween party. Rick's jaw dropped when he saw all the odd people. "It's like another dimension," he said. "We're definitely getting laid here."

After we got drinks Rick went on a rampage. He was usually pretty reserved when it came to initiating conversation with the opposite sex. But since it was "Singles Night," I don't think he felt as vulnerable. His main tactic was to just act like an idiot. Rick started hi-fiving every woman in the gallery. If a girl smiled at him after he bellowed "hi-five", he would start a conversation. Most of the girls Rick hi-fived were ugly, so they smiled back. This meant we had a lot of ugly conversations.

We started talking to two girls. One was decent, and the other was of course chubby. The girls were both co-workers at State Street Bank. Their jobs were boring so we did most of the talking. Rick went into his standard pick up tactics. "You look like Demi Moore," he said to the better looking one, trying to make her feel as pretty as a celebrity.

I decided to keep my mouth shut by not telling the fatty she looked like Michael Moore. Our talk continued and Rick pulled out the number two trick in his pick-up book, the line: "I don't like blow jobs." Most girls fall for it. Even though it sounds awful, the blowjob line usually gets two different but equally positive responses. The girl either thinks she's found Mr. Right, because she hates giving head, or she thinks what the fatty actually said: "You probably haven't gotten a good one."

This usually implies that she's good at giving head and you can expect a free blow job if you hook up. We went back to small talk and in a few minutes a guy came on the loudspeaker announcing the closing of the museum. I wasn't that pissed; we had already found some girls. Now we had to get them to come with us somewhere. "Do you two want to get a drink?" I said.

They looked at each other. The fatty looked interested; the hot chick didn't, but agreed to the plan. We all walked downstairs and the hot one told us to wait in the lobby while they got their coats from the coat check. There was a huge line, but we didn't care. By our late twenties, we were used to waiting around for chicks. We people-watched for about fifteen minutes, which started to feel a little excessive. Rick walked to the coat check to see what was taking so long. He came back with a smile. "Dude, I think we just got ditched," he said.

"They're gone?"

"Dude, no one's there," he said.

I laughed. "Whatever, those girls sucked. What now?"

"I have no idea. We could go to the Dragon. That way we'll be near our place if we meet girls."

"Sure, should we take the Green line?" I said, searching my pocket for enough money to ride the subway. A quarter flew out of my pocket. When I bent over to pick it up, another hand grabbed it first. I stood up to discover a beautiful brunette standing in front of me. "Did you drop this?" she asked.

My eyes connected with hers. They were dark brown, the color of a Hershey bar. She smiled and it felt like a magnet was drawing us together. "I did," I said as we began walking towards each other.

Rick suddenly walked into the middle of our connection. "What are ya, Jewish?" he said to her, being obnoxious.

The girl gave Rick a "what-the-fuck" look. "Was it the nose, or was it the fact that I picked up the quarter?" she said.

I could have killed Rick. He has diarrhea of the mouth, unafraid to rattle off any racial stereotype. "No, you just look Jewish," he said. "No offense."

"I am Jewish," she replied.

"Oh. So is Pile," Rick said, patting me on the back.

The girl laughed at my blonde hair and blue eyes. "You're not Jewish. You're a goyim," she said.

"What does that mean?" I said.

"It just means you're not Jewish," Rick interrupted.

"Don't mind my friend Rick. He says stupid things," I said. "So, um, what are you doing? Are you here all by yourself?"

"I'm with my friend Tracy. She's in the bathroom," she said.

"Do you two want to maybe, like, get a drink?" I said, not even knowing what the other girl looked like.

"We're going to Bondara for a friend's birthday party. You can come if you want. It's not a big deal."

I rolled my eyes at the idea of going to Bondara. That place was full of Boston's elitist tycoons. But there was something about this chick that I liked. I looked at Rick. "Do you want to go?"

"Sure. Who's your friend Tracy?" Rick asked excitedly. Suddenly, a tall, skinny, nerdy girl with Afro hair and big black Buddy Holly glasses walked over to us. Rick rolled his eyes at me. The girl I liked introduced herself as

Alyssa and then introduced us to Tracy. "What was your name again?" Alyssa said to me.

"My name is James."

"His nickname's Pile," Rick said.

"What does that mean?" she asked.

"Pile of shit," Rick responded, laughing.

"Um, I think I'll call you James," Alyssa said to me.

This girl could be a keeper, I thought.

"This is my buddy Rick. But his nickname is 'Dick,'" I said.

"Now that's a fitting nickname," Alyssa said, nodding her head to Rick.

I laughed. She was cool shit, able to take a joke and able to give it right back. "So do you want to get a cab or take the train?" she continued.

"There are four of us. We should just take a cab. It won't cost that much," I said.

Bondara

We hailed a cab and headed over to Bondara. Rick and I gave each other the eye when we walked in, knowing we may be out of our league. In our Old Navy jeans, we looked like we were somebody's poor cousins in town for a wedding. The girls led us to a group of guys dressed in nice collared shirts left slightly unbuttoned to reveal their chests. I hated the unbuttoned shirt look. It always made me wonder where the line was between yuppie and trashy. Alyssa introduced us to the group, who all gave us questionable looks. We were first introduced to Billy, the birthday boy. He was drunk as hell and didn't give a damn about us. The introductions continued until Rick stopped at this metrosexual kid whose eyebrows were as thin as a lunch lady's. "Hey, do you wax your eyebrows?" Rick asked in front of the group.

Everyone was stunned. Rick might as well have hit him over the head with a bottle. "No," the metrosexual kid said with an attitude.

"Yeah you do. Because I did it once and they came out just like that," Rick replied.

"Well, I don't," the metrosexual kid said, sipping of something in a martini glass.

"Okay," Rick said sarcastically.

I was wondering if Rick blew my chances with Alyssa just as I heard a faint laugh from her mouth. She sat down and quickly changed the topic to Billy's birthday. Tracy apparently didn't care about Rick insulting the metrosexual, because she asked him twenty questions as quickly as the Micro Machine man. "So Rick, where do you live?" Tracy said.

"The North End," he said, annoyed.

"Do you have any roommates?"

"Yeah, Pile," Rick said.

"Oh that must be fun! Where do you work?"

"Some insurance company."

"Oh, what do you do there?'

"Sit at a desk."

"Do you have a girlfriend?"

Rick looked over at me. "Dude, we got to go," he said quietly.

I gave him the puppy dog eyes. "Dude, just hang in there. I like this Alyssa girl."

"She's not even talking to you anymore," Rick pointed out.

He was right, and there were a bunch of pretty boys surrounding her. Usually, I would just cut my losses, but I felt like I had to hang in there. When one of the guys next to Alyssa left for the bathroom, the metrosexual guy moved into his place and started whispering something in her ear. I knew it was about us. I looked over at Rick and he saw it too. "Dude, it's over. You know he's talking about us," Rick said.

"I'm sure. You basically called him a fag in front of all his friends."

Rick laughed. "Look at his drink, he is a fag. What do you think he's saying about us?"

"Stay away from these kids. They're trouble," I said in a faggy accent.

Rick continued the imitation game. "If you want to go slumming, you should date my hairdresser. At leased he can offer you free waxings," Rick said in his own gay accent.

We drank our beers and soon everyone began to clear out. I looked at my watch – it was only eleven o'clock. The group all said goodbye to Alyssa and Tracy but the only one who said anything to us was Billy the birthday boy. He shook our hands and thanked us for coming. It was nice. I thought he was an asshole like his friends, but I was wrong.

It was now just the four of us, and I was pretty happy to get a chance to talk to Alyssa. I bought a round of drinks and was pleased when Alyssa ordered a beer and not a fancy drink. "So what's up with those guys?" I asked her.

"I only like Billy. He's an old friend. The rest think they're better than everyone else. But if their parents weren't paying for their condos. they'd be living at home."

I laughed and asked Alyssa about her life. She told me she was a nurse and lived in Cambridge. I was nervous when I told her about my late-twenties college lifestyle but she didn't think anything of it. "Enjoy it. I would do anything to go back," she said.

179

"You should."

"Maybe someday," she said, taking a sip of beer.

I looked over to Rick, who was still battling his way through a conversation with Tracy. Alyssa mentioned that Tracy lived in the same apartment building as her, and I saw right away that this was going to be a problem. I needed a way to find a way back to Alyssa's house, which meant Rick would have to play along.

As my connection with Alyssa grew stronger, I realized I needed Rick more than ever. When the girls started talking to each other about tennis, I leaned towards Rick. "So are you going to jump on the grenade for me, or what?"

"You're a fucking asshole. You're going to make me fuck that bug-eyed chick. Dude, she's got an Afro!" he said.

"I really like Alyssa and think I've got a shot, but someone's gonna have to get with Aphrodite," I said.

Rick paused for a second, then put his arm behind Tracy's chair. He mouthed the words, "You owe be big time for this," then started flirting with Tracy.

Why We Jump On The Grenade

I started to flirt more heavily with Alyssa and before you knew it, it was last call. We got up and started to walk out of the bar. I was worried that Rick would back out. He and I fell back behind the girls. "I'm bringing Aphrodite back to our place," Rick said. "Are you happy?"

I was relieved, but still had to figure out my approach with Alyssa. I could bring her back to our apartment but my room hadn't been cleaned since I moved in. If Alyssa was a slampig, I wouldn't have cared and just did it on my dirty laundry but she wasn't.

"How am I going to get back to Alyssa's house?" I said to Rick.

"Just bring her back to our place," Rick said.

"No, my rooms a mess," I said.

"See why it's important to 'not' be a slob," Rick lectured me.

"Whatever, lets not start this," I said referring to Rick being the bitch of the house.

"Dude, if you don't go back there, I'm aborting the Aphrodite mission," Rick said.

We caught up to the girls and Rick moved in on Aphrodite, so I could invite myself over to Alyssa's. I didn't know what to say so I resorted to old tactics. "So Alyssa, do you want to like, give me the tour of Cambridge?" I asked.

It sounded so bad. I knew it wouldn't stick. "That's the worst line I've ever heard," she said laughing.

I was about to give the signal for Rick to abort his mission, then Alyssa said, "You can come back if you want. My building has a ping pong table. We should play."

I couldn't believe it, I was in. As the girls hailed a cab I whispered to Rick, "Hey, I'm in. Thank you so much. Sorry you have to hook up with that Aphrodite."

"Fuck it," Rick said. "A lay's a lay."

We each got our own cabs. When Alyssa and I arrived at her apartment building she actually split the fare with me. We didn't play ping pong, which was just as well. I think she just said that so she wouldn't look like a slut. We sat on the couch in her apartment watching the late night news on repeat. I finally got up my courage and leaned in to kiss Alyssa. She kissed back, very soft and gentle. We made out for a few minutes and I wanted to take it to the next level. I reached up her shirt and under her bra to massage her breasts. They felt good. I started to unbutton her belt, when her hand slammed down on mine like a bear trap. "Let's wait," she said.

The times I had gotten the "let's wait" line before, I usually just waited another three minutes before trying again. But this time I didn't. I liked and respected this girl. It wasn't just because of how she had acted during the night; I felt something about her that I had never felt from first meeting a woman.

I slept at her house and we went to breakfast in the morning. Again, she split the tab with me. This was an amazing streak of luck. We went our separate ways and on my train ride back to the apartment, I called Rick to thank him for jumping on the grenade. "You're welcome, I think..." Rick said.

"What do you mean?"

"Aphrodite was a spaz in bed."

I laughed. "That's good right?"

"I'm not sure I'll ever be the same." He laughed insecurely. "She stuck her finger in my ass."

"That's fucking gross."

"Did you bang that chick Alyssa?" Rick asked.

"No, but we hooked up. I liked her. I'm going to try and date her."

"Whatever, if you think I'm doubling with you, you're fucking crazy. I'm all set with Aphrodite and her busy finger," Rick said.

The next night I ended up hanging out with Alyssa and her "real" friends, not those trendy people from Bondaro. They were all really funny and I liked them a lot. Having your chick's friends pass the cool test is one of the most important things in a relationship. If they suck, the relationship will never work, because you'd be stuck hanging out with miserable people the whole time.

182

When we got back to Alyssa's house, again, we didn't have sex. She wanted to wait. I was upset at this '50s style dating, but she was worth it. We had a few more dates and finally, she put out. The sex was amazing. It seemed to last for hours. When I hooked up with a slampig, I'd usually give her the two-pumps-and-dump, then think of a way to get the fuck out of dodge. But since I liked Alyssa, I could last. When I finally came, I didn't have that feeling of shame that I was used to.

11

AIDS Test

Thanks to MapQuest, I found the walk-in clinic in Lynn, Massachusetts. Being a white, suburban kid, I was unfamiliar with the city of Lynn. All I really knew of it was from a rhyme: "Lynn, Lynn, city of sin. Never come out, the way you came in." That day the rhyme felt truer than ever; I was at the walk-in clinic to get an AIDS test.

Walking through the automatic doors, I wasn't sure why I was there. Even though I had spent the majority of my twenties banging chicks I met at dive bars and after-parties, I had never considered getting tested. Whenever I watched a PSA or saw a poster telling me to "get tested," I disregarded it. I figured if I ever did get the "HIV" I would go out with a bang like Eazy-E. One day you're on top of your game, the next you're dead.

I had been involved with Alyssa for over six months, an all-time record for me. She was drop dead gorgeous, yet not a controlling bitch like most hot chicks. People like Alyssa were one in a million. I was in love. But there's just one catch to falling in love: you have to be open and honest about your past. Now honesty didn't necessarily mean I was going to tell her about the warthog I fucked in a porta potty at an AC/DC concert. But it did mean offering a summarized version: "I have made some poor choices in my life."

That's all Alyssa had to hear. She told me that if I wanted to have unprotected sex with her I would have to get an AIDS test. She added, "It isn't just for sexual purposes; it's for future committal reasons, too."

So there I was, at the Lynn walk-in clinic. The reason I chose such a horrible place to get tested was for two reasons. One, my student health insurance didn't pick up the bill for AIDS tests. And two, the whole thing was anonymous. Apparently, if you get tested at your regular doctor and have AIDS you have to register yourself like a sex offender.

When my number was called, I walked up to a receptionist. She was a smoking hot black girl who couldn't have been over 23. I sat down on a hard plastic seat while she looked me up and down. I clearly didn't belong there. "What brings you in today, sir?" she said.

"I'm here for an AIDS test. I hear it's free," I said, choosing my words poorly.

She looked at me like I was an asshole. The Lynn walk-in clinic was filled with illegal immigrants with no health care. They were probably bleeding in the waiting room because they hurt themselves cutting some rich guy's lawn. Here I was, some white-bread suburban kid, looking for a freebie. The receptionist smirked. "Our AIDS tests are free of charge and anonymous. If you could fill out this form, one of our nurses will be with you as soon as possible."

I got up from the plastic chair to take the clipboard and form from her. When I turned, I saw my seat had been taken by a woman with a baby in her arms. I sighed and filled out the form standing up. Although the receptionist said the test was anonymous, I still wrote my alias, "Steve Crowley," on the form. I used that name when I got caught shoplifting from Spencer Gifts as a kid.

About an hour after passing in my perjured form, a nurse came out to call my fake name. She was a heavy-set Hispanic woman with braids in her hair. "Hi Steve," she said as she looked at the clipboard. "I'm Rosita. Come with me to the lab."

She sped up my visit by asking the standard questions as we walked together down the hallway. "Do you drink, smoke, do drugs, sleep with prostitutes?"

I said no to everything but drink. In the lab Rosita didn't waste any time. She put me in a chair and had my arm in a rubber tourniquet fifteen seconds later. When a vein formed she began to draw blood, filling the vial. Rosita took the needle out of my arm, discarded it, and slapped a sticker on the vial. That was it. She then handed me a business card with a series of numbers on it. "Come back in two weeks and your results will be in."

"Where do I go?" I asked.

"Go to the receptionist in the front room. Not the back where you were before. The front. Give her the card, she'll know what to do."

Before I could leave, Rosita had disappeared into another room and returned with a bulgy unsealed envelope. "These are for you," she said.

I took the envelope and opened up the flap. Inside were eight to ten condoms. I could feel my face turn red as I looked up at Rosita. She had a big grin on her face. "These are really good," she said and gave me a wink.

That night, when my girlfriend and I were getting it on, I pulled out one of Rosita's rubbers. Sliding it over the tip of my penis, I realized it was extra small. It felt like a rubber band tied around my penis. I took the condom off before my penis turned blue with suffocation. Rosita must have given me the extra small rubbers because I was a white guy.

While I waited for my test results, I thought back to some of the late night Altered Beasts I'd slept with. I got kind of aroused just thinking about the adventure of going after them. I kept asking myself the same questions over and over. Was I really ready for the next step? Was I ready to spend the rest of my life banging the same chick, then watching HGTV?

AIDS Test Results

Two weeks later the results were in, waiting for me at the walk-in clinic. Most men who've had their AIDS tests will tell stories of biting their nails the entire two-week wait. But I figured, why worry about something you can't change?

If I did have AIDS, I would have to deal with it. I just hoped that I hadn't accidentally spread anything to Alyssa. She was such a good girl and didn't deserve the scarlet letter across her vagina.

I luckily found a parking spot outside the clinic. This was key since I didn't want to park a few blocks away at the Big Lots. A few blocks in this section of Lynn was a few too many for a slice of Wonder Bread like myself. I got out of my car and hit the automatic lock on my key chain. "Well, here goes nothing," I said aloud.

Two automatic doors opened up in front of me and I hoped I wouldn't have to wait as long as I had before. When I walked up to the receptionist's booth I passed by a man and a pregnant girl. The girl looked 16 and the guy looked like he was 60. I hoped he wasn't her baby's daddy.

The receptionist was on the phone yelling at someone in Spanish. I couldn't make out what she was saying but I was pretty sure "puta" was the Spanish word for bitch. Maybe she was on the phone with a veterinarian.

She saw me and quickly hung up the phone. She looked me up and down with a big smile. "How can I help you this morning?"

I figured the sudden change of attitude meant she thought I was the new med student intern. I pulled out the card Rosita had given me. "I have this card. I'm here for my results or something," I said.

She took the card, looked at it, and dialed an extension. She talked in Spanish to whoever was on the other end and hung up the phone. "The counselor will be out to see you shortly," she said.

That statement gave me a shiver. The nail-biting AIDS paranoia had finally hit me. I could actually have AIDS. My whole life would be ruined. No wedding bells and rugrats running around calling me Daddy. I was doomed.

I broke into a sweat and started pacing back and forth. A crackhead stood up from the water fountain and patted me on the shoulder. "You alright man?" he said.

"I'm fine, just a little um..."

The crackhead interrupted. "You look like you're having a bad trip. My man, you needs to sit down."

I nodded my head. "That sounds like a good idea."

I sat down next to the 16-year-old pregnant girl and ran my fingers through my sweaty hair. A feeling overtook me that I had not felt in years. It was the same anxiety I had felt after fucking Grimace in Club Boom. Remembering what I had done back then to get myself together, I went to the bathroom.

I threw water on my face and entered the handicapped stall. After a few seconds of telling myself I would be alright, I realized a pep talk wouldn't calm me down this time. All I kept asking myself was, "Why would I need to see a counselor? Couldn't they just give me an envelope with the results?"

There was a good chance that I had AIDS and my life had just turned into an ABC special. So I did what most people do when they are fucked. I looked to God. I kneeled down in front of the toilet, cupped my hands together and began to pray. I don't remember what exactly I said, but it was pretty much like everyone else's prayers – trying to get something you don't deserve.

I went back to the lobby and found my seat next to the pregnant girl. The next five minutes felt like fifty. Time dragged on like a bad act at a high school talent show. Then Rosita came out of the back room. Apparently she was a nurse and a counselor. She had a white envelope in her hand which I presumed were the results. "Steve, nice to see you again," she said.

I almost corrected her, then remembered my alias. She saw me trembling. "Are you okay?" she said. "You're pale. We need to get you some water."

"I'm okay, let's just get this over with," I said.

"I see. We're going to have to go into one of the counseling rooms for privacy."

Again, I knew something wrong. Why couldn't she hand me the envelope and let me just go about my business? It was because I was going to need a counselor when I found out I was HIV-positive.

We walked into a bare room with only a table, phone, and two chairs. We sat down across from each other. My right knee noticeably shook up and down.

"Steve, you need to relax. Tell me, why are you acting this way?"

I just wanted her to tell me if I had AIDS or not. I didn't want her to talk to me about anything else. "Do you know my results?" I asked.

She paused for a second. "I do. But there are some procedures we need to go through before I can give them to you," she said.

"Procedures? Why? Why do we need to go through procedures?" I cried.

She put her hand on my knee. "Steve, you need to calm down. If you don't, I can't give you the results. Now Steve, I am going to try one last time. Tell me, why do you feel that you are at risk?"

I slammed my fist on the table. "Because, I've spent my life fucking slampigs! Ugly chicks, fat chicks, old chicks, crazy chicks and worst of all, trashy chicks. I fucked em all! That's why! Now just give me the fucking results!"

Rosita rolled her eyes. "It's negative. You can love yourself again."

I felt like I had just taken a hit off a crack pipe. I was in an instant euphoria.

"Were you just fucking with me for your own personal amusement?" I asked.

Rosita laughed. "That's what everyone says," she said. "I know, it's a bad procedure."

Before leaving the clinic, I had Rosita photocopy the results so I could hang them on my refrigerator like a good test score. I hugged her goodbye. The future was mine. I 'was' ready to bang the same chick for the rest of my life, even if it did involve watching HGTV. When we were ready, I was going to ask for her hand. I felt like the luckiest person in the world and wasn't going to take it for granted.

12

The Real Test

Ten Years Earlier

Back when I was in high school, I sat next to a girl named Jen in algebra class. With one glance, you could tell she was a slampig. She was the girl who had a story circulating about her every other day. Her full name was Jennifer Sampson. She got around so much, the kids nicknamed her Jen Slampson.

Despite her promiscuous ways, Jen Slampson and I became friendly. There was a certain glamour to her vulnerability that I liked, not to mention her glossy pink lipstick and "accidentally" unbuttoned blouse. On the nights Jen wasn't getting gang-banged by our high school football team, she would be up talking on the phone with me. We didn't just talk on the phone either; we hung out.

One day I sat in a smoking circle with my friends and Jen's name came up. "Pile, you hitting that?" Scotty asked.

"No, not yet," I said, looking down in shame.

"You're with her all the time and you haven't even fucked her? Dude, you're a fucking homo," he said.

The truth was that I had never had sex. That lie I told about sleeping with the girl up at the beach was starting to wear thin. I wanted to lose the big V, but didn't know how to. Like most guys who are in a rush to lose their virginity, I decided to try for the slampig. Because of my friendly connection with Jen and her whorish ways, I figured she was sure to have sex with me.

It was a late night at this girl Amanda's party and I had brought Jen down to the basement to smoke a joint. When it was down to a roach, I put it out and an awkward silence came over us. I knew it was now or never. I went in for the kiss. Jen quickly put her hand up the way a school crossing guard would. "You're my friend. I don't want to ruin our friendship," she said.

"Oh, okay. Sorry," I said and looked the other way.

"Its okay, hun," Jen said as she slapped my knee. "Hey, I got to go pee. I'll be right back. We'll smoke a butt!"

Jen stood up and walked upstairs. After waiting by myself for about five minutes, I decided to go upstairs to look for her. I didn't see her in the living room or kitchen so I decided to check the back porch. Maybe she smoked a butt without me. When I opened the door, there was Jen making out with Chad Stevens, a guy who had once dumped beer on her head.

Jen rejected me that night, not because I wasn't good-looking or as cool as Chad Stevens, but because I was friends with her. This made me the "Emotional Rag Doll," otherwise known as the "Fag Friend." You like someone, and she likes you back – as a friend. She could be treated like a princess, but no, she would rather be treated like a piece of meat.

Slampig

As the stories of Jen Slampson's promiscuous ways continued, I grew more discouraged. It was like hearing your friends talk about the new violent video game that you never played because your mom was a hippie.

One day I decided I'd had enough and made the only power play a guy could. I cut her out of my life. You know what they say: if you love something, let it go. If it comes back, it's yours. So I did. Then I got older and just laughed at the stories about Jen Slampson, but never added to them.

Ten Years Later

My relationship with Alyssa was two years in and going strong. Sure, there were rough patches when I felt like leaving and going back to pigging, but where would that leave me?

When Rick and I went out together, we were constantly getting hit on. Probably because we both had girlfriends. Having a relationship is odd. You spend years being lonely and spanking it to the girl who served you chicken wings. But then you get into a relationship, and any girl with a few Appletinis in her wants to bang you. I was smart, though. When I had that chance to hook up, I didn't. It was just like quitting smoking, then jonesing for a butt. You might want it, but you've already abstained for so long, the relapse isn't worth it. Rick, on the other hand, had a double life and took advantage of the situation.

After work, Rick and I frequently met up for beers at a bar in the Faneuil Hall area called Dirty D's. Normally I would turn my nose up at those meathead bars, but Dirty D's had dollar drafts. Shit, I'd drink at a bingo parlor for dollar drafts. As usual, Rick and I were poking fun at every idiot in the place. Then I heard some girls' voices come from the door behind me and looked. It was Jennifer Sampson, my former high school obsession. If I had a most wanted list for slampigs, Jen would be number one, right next to Courtney Love. There was a difference in the Jen Slampson I knew in high school and the one who just walked into the bar. This one was smoking hot.

I nudged Rick. "Look who just walked in."

Rick looked back. "Oh shit, Jen Slampson. Didn't you used to fuck her in high school?"

"No, I didn't get the chance."

"Here's your chance," Rick said.

"Whatever, I have a girlfriend stupid. Some of us have morals."

"I'll fuck her than," Rick said.

Jen spotted me right away and waved as she walked over. Her face seemed to get better as she got closer. Trailing behind her was a short girl with dirty blonde hair – definitely fuckable. "Oh wait, looks like I'm gonna need a wingman," Rick said.

Jen gave Rick and me one of those half-hugs that girls tend to give and introduced us to her friend Lisa. The bartender jumped off her stool in back where she had been munching down mozzarella sticks and came over to take the girls' orders. Jen ordered two frozen mudslides, which was weird. Dirty D's was only good for pouring, not blending.

The bartender cleaned off the blender. It probably hadn't been used since Dirty D's first opened. "Do you know where we are?" I asked Jen.

"Yeah, why?" she replied.

"We're at Dirty D's. This isn't Starbucks. Order a fucking beer. Or at least a Captain and coke."

"I can order a Captain and coke any day. Today, I'm celebrating."

"Celebrating what?" I asked.

"My last day working at the collection agency. I'm moving to Idaho."

"Moving to Idaho? Sounds more like you should be mourning instead."

Jen gave me a light push. "You ass," she said.

The drinks came out and looked like milk shakes. Rick laughed. "What are we in a 50's diner?"

The bartender smiled. "I know, I should have a poodle skirt on," she said.

Jen pulled out her credit card and Lisa took money out of her pocket, slowly, like you do when out to dinner with your father. Jen waved her free hand while giving the card to the bartender. "Don't worry about it, hun."

"Glad I'm not paying for those things," Rick said.

I looked at Jen. "Some celebration. You're buying your own drinks. Do you buy yourself a cake on your birthday too?" I said like an asshole.

"You're a jerk. I haven't seen you for years and this is how you act. We can sit somewhere else if you like," she said, not finding me amusing.

"Relax. I was just fucking around," I said, giving her a pat on the shoulder.

Later, after many drinks and ignored texts from my girlfriend, I was shit-faced. The girls were heavily flirting with us. We were flirting back, but because we had girlfriends, we didn't give it much effort. For me, it was just to know that I was still alive. It's really hypocritical of us guys because if we saw our girlfriends even asking a guy for directions, we would be bullshit.

Rick bought a round of Jameson shots and we put them back. "Yow," I said and slammed the shot glass onto the table.

"Your girlfriend is a lucky woman. You've matured into a great catch," Jen said with a smile.

"I always was a great catch," I said, taking a sip of my beer.

"I know," Jen said as she put her hand on my leg.

The booze was surging through my bloodstream and I suddenly felt an urge I had not felt since high school. I wanted Jen Slampson. I wanted to ride the pony everyone else had ridden. She definitely wanted to hook up too. But why did she want to hook up now, and not back in the day? It was most likely a combination of my "I don't give a fuck attitude" plus having a girlfriend. It's real sick how girls are attracted to guys with girlfriends. I'm not saying we men are saints, but we usually walk away from girls who say they are in a relationship. Girls are drawn to guys who are involved. It's almost like they're thinking, "He has a girlfriend so he must be doing something right."

"I'm really glad we got to hang out before I leave. It's been so long since I've seen you," Jen said, batting her eyes.

She took a sip from her third frozen mudslide and lightly licked her lips. "Do you want to go out for a cigarette?" she asked.

She was using the old "go out for a smoke so we can make out" tactic. Unfortunately for her, I had quit cigarettes and slampigs a number of years ago.

"I don't smoke butts anymore," I said.

"Will you come outside with me so I don't have to be alone?" she asked, batting her eyes again.

I needed some fresh air from the Dirty D's stench of Axe and cheap perfume, so I agreed. But, even though Jen used to be a main character in my "Spank Bank," hooking up with her wasn't worth it. I did, however, have an ulterior motive in going outside with her. I would lead her on, let her make a move, and then laugh in her face. I would have my revenge by leaving Jen wet and upset. As I walked out with Jen, Rick winked at me because he thought I was going to cheat on my girlfriend the way he did on his. I shook my head, signaling that I wasn't. He, being a positive influence, mouthed the word "pussy" as I followed Jen out.

Outside, Jen lit up her cigarette and blew the smoke in my face. I didn't really care; I like the smell of secondhand smoke. I started to bring up our glory years as teenagers in our hometown. "Those were some really good times," she said, trying to force a moment by looking in my eyes.

Then my revenge plan started to unravel: I was getting horny. Sure, I had told myself that I wouldn't touch her. But when it's right in front of you, how can you resist? Then I thought of how great my girlfriend was, and wondered whether Jen Slampson was worth it.

A homeless guy walked up to us and rattled his cup in our face. I gave him attitude, but I was glad he snapped me out of my lust. I wasn't going to hook up with Jen. She lost her chance years ago. I started to walk away and Jen put her right hand on the side of my rib cage. "Pile, kiss me."

My penis went from half a stalk to full bamboo stick and I lost my senses again. There she was. The slampig of my dreams was creaming her panties for me and I had to make a decision. "I can't, I'm with someone," I said.

She dropped her cigarette and grasped the other side of my rib cage. "Your girlfriend's not here and I'm leaving for Idaho. Let's just see what happens."

I stopped for a second and thought. Jen was right; my girlfriend wasn't here and would never find out. I could totally get away with cheating. Jen pushed me up against the brick wall; her crotch pressed against my hard penis. "Pile, I know you've always wanted me. Here's your chance."

Jen closed her eyes. This was it, the ultimate test. I put my hands on her rib cage and leaned in. I tilted my head, moving my mouth towards hers, and we gently kissed. I could taste the chocolaty drink she had been slurping down throughout the night. Jen started massaging my back. I grabbed her ribs tighter and the kissing got heavier. She pulled away. "Mmm, that was nice," Jen whispered.

I wanted to fuck her so bad. "Where are you staying tonight?" I asked.

"At my parent's house. Can we go back to your apartment?" Jen asked.

That was a possibility, but I didn't want to risk it. God forbid my girlfriend found a blonde pubic hair in my bed. So I made the decision.

I grabbed her hand and led her into the small alley between Dirty D's and another bar. We walked behind a green dumpster and resumed kissing. Trash day must have been the next morning because it was overflowing with garbage. All I could smell was rotting food. Jen seemed unaffected by the stench. She must have been too drunk to notice or had smoked her sense of smell away. I slid my hand inside her pants touching her ass. It wasn't a surprise that she had a thong on. A slut like Jen had probably been wearing thongs since eighth grade.

Jen stopped kissing me and started sucking my ear. I loved it. I took my free hand and used my thumb to rub her hard nipples poking out of her tank top. Jen undid my belt and started stroking my solid cock up and down. "I want you to fuck me," she said.

"Do you have a condom?" I said.

Slampig

"No, but I'm on birth control," Jen said.

I was so drunk I didn't care. My only hope was she had taken the pill religiously and didn't miss a day. I grabbed an old cardboard box that once held tomato paste out of the dumpster and flattened it with my foot. Jen lay on the box and pulled her jeans and thong down to her ankles. I leaned over her and inserted my cock. Going in felt so good, mainly because I knew it was so wrong.

With every pump she breathed heavier and heavier. Then I could feel my penis pulsing. I was about to cum. I pulled out just in time, and squirted all over her vagina and stomach. I was immediately ashamed of myself. I had done it again. I had fucked a slampig. I looked at Jen. She was soaked in cum, lying on a flattened cardboard box, in an alley full of rotting trash. This was exactly where she belonged.

I climbed off her and pulled my pants up. She riffled through her purse and took out some Dunkin Donuts napkins and proceeded to mop up my giz. After getting herself together, we walked out of the alley. "Wow, that was classy" Jen said.

My eyes started to water. I had learned nothing over the years. I needed to get Rick and get out of this situation. He would straighten me out with a "it's not cheating if you're not married" pep talk. I took my cell phone out of my back pocket to look at the time. It read "Alyssa connected". My stomach dropped, I must have pocket dialed my girlfriend by mistake. The call duration continued to climb 12:42, 12:43, 12:44 and I deserved every second of it.

About Pile

Pile is a Stand-Up Comedian from the Merrimack Valley of Massachusetts. His main influences are the people he grew up with. Pile feels that the real comedians are our friends, family, and co-workers whose life stories are funnier than anything a comedian could make up. In June of 2008, Pile won a comedy competition where he had to perform in front of two-hundred rowdy people. He credits this mostly from spending numerous hours practicing his act at bars, where barely anyone is paying attention. Pile is dyslexic and practically illiterate so he thanks all the people who helped him edit this book. Feel free to email him with comments, complaints and if you find any errors in this book. You can do this at Slampigbook@gmail.com or go to his facebook at www.facebook.com/Slampigbook. If you are interested in booking Pile for an appearance you can email Pileproductions@gmail.com .

Special Thanks

Special thanks to Mina and Lynz, for the gutter work edits. Rick for helping me with my punch lines. Faucher, Jimmy W, and Daddy Warbucks, for the clean ups. Scotty L, for the first edition printing. Kate Crandell for the cover. MG and KL, for final edits. MVM post for letting me record the audio book. And Rich for the stickers.

Thank you all!

Made in the USA
Middletown, DE
29 January 2020